CURATORS'
CHOICE

CURATORS' CHOICE

An Introduction to the Art Museums of the U.S.

BY BABBETTE BRANDT FROMME

CROWN PUBLISHERS, INC.   NEW YORK

Inquiries should be addressed to Crown Publishers, Inc., One Park Avenue, New York, New York 10016
Printed in the United States of America
Published simultaneously in Canada by General Publishing Company Limited

Library of Congress Cataloging in Publication Data
Fromme, Babbette Brandt.
   Curators' choice—Western edition.

   1. Art—The West.   2. Art museums—The West.
I. Title.
N510.5.W4F76   1981   708.18   80-17772
ISBN: 0-517-542005

Designed by Deborah B. Kerner

10 9 8 7 6 5 4 3 2 1
First Edition

FOR OLIVER FORMATO

CONTENTS

FOREWORD

Museums are important cultural resources in America. Their collections span a broad spectrum, from world famous masterpieces to works of art of regional significance. The scholar and specialist, through long study and access to museum archives, know the locations of the objects in which they have a particular professional interest wherever they are scattered among our nation's museums. On the other hand, the art lover who visits a city may be unaware of the riches of the local museum or other nearby collections. This book, *Curators' Choice,* has been written to fill a long-felt need fc ˉ a reference guide to the art collections of America. Such a vast undertaking wisely has been organized into regional sections.

You as a private collector or avid museumgoer undoubtedly know quite well the museum of your hometown. But, when you visit another city will you know all the museums that you may wish to visit and what their specialities are? The author, Babbette Brandt Fromme, having long worked in museums, recognized that the best way of summarizing a museum's collection is to entrust the task to the actual curators of the various institutions. Accordingly, she asked the staffs of the museums to make a curator's choice of the objects of art in their museums that typify the collections, and that should be on a "Don't Miss" list.

We are all accustomed to the books that are museum guides, but here is a book that is a guide to museums.

> Joseph Veach Noble
> *Director, Museum of the City of New York*
> *Past President, American Association of Museums*

PREFACE

Often, on entering a museum for the first time, I found myself eagerly wondering, What are its strengths? Are my special interests represented? What should I definitely try to see? There is always so little time, and it is so easy to get tired and miss things you later regret. So many others feel this way too that I embarked upon this guide. Its aim: to furnish the museumgoer with a sampling of the collections so as to heighten his or her enjoyment of the actual time spent in the museum. I want to stress that this is only a representative sampling, the tip of the iceberg, so to speak, compiled with the interested but unprofessional viewer in mind.

The selections are not mine but have been made by the directors, the curators or other experts in each museum. The descriptions of the objects were either supplied by the museums or culled from books on the particular subject.

Where no gallery locations are given next to an object, it is because (a) the museum is small enough to make this unnecessary, (b) the item is in storage waiting to be rotated for exhibition or (c) it is out on loan.

Museums today are living entities and are constantly growing and changing. Therefore it is virtually impossible to keep totally abreast of each museum's facilities, hours and admissions. A phone call made just before your visit might spare you possible disappointment.

There is a great deal publicly available for our pleasure in the world of art. I hope this book makes it easier for you to find your way among the centuries of artistic treasures so generously represented in the museums in this country.

ACKNOWLEDGMENTS

One of the nicest dividends derived from collating the material in these books was the enthusiasm and generous support I enjoyed. Museum personnel throughout the country expressed their approval by offering the information I requested and taking time to check the finished copy.

During the lengthy time it took me to complete the project, my husband was always available for guidance. This involved long discussions on the manuscript as well as frequent interruptions of his own work with questions to which he unfailingly responded with good cheer. He endured many hours on dull roads to reach museums of real interest (to him) and assumed more than his share of household tasks in order to free my time.

The members of the Public Information Department at the Metropolitan Museum of Art made their expertise available to me and opened doors to other sources when needed, always expressing keen interest in my project. For this I am grateful to John Ross, Berenice Heller, Richard Pierce, Joan Ingalls and Joan Gould. My special thanks are offered to Jack Frizzelle, the department's director, who encouraged me to undertake this job in the first place when its size and practical problems suggested that I scotch the effort.

It was a pleasure to work with Betty Brandt (no relation) who spent many hours in libraries, relentlessly tracking down dates and obscure facts, while maintaining a sense of humor.

I felt always able to call upon my good friend Norma Rayman when additional research help was required. Her company on a variety of junkets made the work a pleasure.

My own compliments and those of my publishers go to Gilda Charwat and Dorothy Edwards for typing this very complex manuscript almost entirely free of error. Always available and deeply committed to the work, they turned what could have been a nightmare into a joy.

Crown Publishers themselves deserve special mention; they were never discouraged by either the enormity of this task or its esoteric sections: Herb Michelman who provided me with the opportunity to publish these books; Rosemary Baer, production editor, for example, seemed always more willing the more difficult the problems; finally, my editor, Brandt Aymar, who guided me through the complexities of this undertaking with great open-mindedness and without drama: "Thank you, Brandt."

WESTERN EDITION

CURATORS' CHOICE

NOME

CARRIE McCLAIN MEMORIAL MUSEUM
Front St.
Nome, AK 99762
Tel: (907)443-5242

The museum's collection was inaugurated with original photographs and artifacts of early Nome amassed by Carrie McClain. She lived in Nome for most
of her life and became its City Clerk. A new floor, a recent addition to the
building, has doubled the exhibition space.

SAMPLING THE COLLECTION

PHOTOGRAPH COLLECTION

Hundreds of old photographs depict the early residents and life-style of the
Nome area.

IVORY CARVINGS

The collection includes examples of both new ivory and old mastodon ivory
exhibiting different techniques used by carvers. A slide show depicts styles and
methods of carving.

NATIVE ESKIMO ART

This collection includes all phases of Eskimo art: carvings, block prints, sketches,
skin clothing, wood carvings, ceremonial masks and basketry.

GOLD RUSH ARTIFACTS

Many examples of gold-mining equipment and techniques are displayed. Min-
ing artifacts include sluices, rockers, picks, shovels and scales from the Nome
gold rush.

FACILITIES

On Sale are duplications of the museum's photographs, which are moderately
priced.

Hours: *Winter hours:* Monday, Wednesday, 10 A.M.–8 P.M.; Tuesday, Thursday, Friday, 10 A.M.–5 P.M. Saturday, 10 A.M.–4 P.M. *Closed:* Sundays,
legal holidays. *Call for summer hours.*

Admission: Free.

SITKA

SHELDON JACKSON MUSEUM
Sheldon Jackson College
Sitka, AK 99835
Tel: (907)747-5228

This octagonal one-room museum boasts the state's oldest collection. Housed in the first concrete building to be erected in Alaska, it features objects from the everyday life of the aboriginal Eskimos, Aleuts, Athapaskans and Southeast Alaska Indians.

SAMPLING THE COLLECTION

METLAKATLA   *2 Mortuary Totem Poles*
These poles were built to honor important persons. One is a storytelling pole and the other a house post and are among the oldest to be seen anywhere.

OLD CULTURE, ALEUT   *Lamp*
                                            Stone
This lamp is thought to be centuries old. It was made by pecking and polishing, a technique used in the Neolithic period, and is lit with whale oil.

ALEUT   *Card Case*
                                            Rye grass
The fine craftsmanship of Aleut women is exhibited in their basketry. Made expressly as souvenirs during the gold rush, these cases were prized by wealthy miners who paid high prices for them.

ESKIMO   *Whaler's Suit*
Point Barrow
One of the rarest pieces in the collection, this skin suit resembles a modern jumpsuit.

**Left of
Entrance**   HAIDA INDIAN   *Canoe*
                                            prior to 1830
                                            Argillite (slate or shale)
The carving on this canoe of a shaman, or medicine man, on a vision quest shows the influence of the Europeans and their ships on the Haida artists.

FACILITIES

Walking Tours are available.

The *Sales Desk* offers postcards, bulletins, catalogs and other publications; also slides of artifacts and Sitka scenes at 50¢ each or 3 for $1, lithographs of Alaskan peoples, 35¢ each, or 6 for $2.

Hours: *Summer:* Daily, June 1–September 15, 8 A.M.–5 P.M. *Winter:* Phone for hours.

Admission: Adults, $1; children, free.

ARIZONA

PHOENIX

**HEARD MUSEUM
22 East Monte Vista Rd.
Phoenix, AZ 85004
Tel: (602)252-8848**

The Heard Museum is devoted to anthropology and primitive art. The major emphasis of the museum is on the prehistory and history of the Southwest, with special attention given to the Native American peoples inhabiting this area. Its collections also extend beyond these limits to include primitive arts from the cultures of Africa, Asia and Oceania. Since the exhibits change often, the museum is able to display a sizable portion of its permanent collection on a rotating basis. It is therefore not possible to select outstanding examples that are always on view.

FACILITIES

Guided Tours, Lectures and *Films* are available.

The *Gift Shop* sells the finest authentic Southwestern Indian rugs, pottery, silver and basketry and has added a wider selection of items, such as Hopi kachina dolls and Seri woodcarvings. The quality remains high but the price range now allows more people the opportunity to purchase fine Native American crafts.

Hours: Monday–Saturday, 10 A.M.–5 P.M. Sunday, 1 P.M.–5 P.M. *Closed:* National holidays.

Admission: Adults, $1.50; senior citizens, $1; children and students, 50¢.

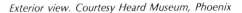

Exterior view. Courtesy Heard Museum, Phoenix

PHOENIX ART MUSEUM
1625 North Central Ave.
Phoenix, AZ 85004
Tel: (602)257-1222

This contemporary-style museum building overlooks a courtyard of tasteful plantings and playing fountains. Last year more than 250,000 visitors inspected its collection, which ranges from the Renaissance to the present. Its major strengths are 18th-century French painting, contemporary art, Western American art and an exhibit of blue and white Chinese porcelains. Additionally, the Mexican art collection, the Thorne Miniature Rooms and the Arizona Costume Institute are of interest to view.

SAMPLING THE COLLECTION

Renaissance Gallery   FRENCH   *Princes and Martyrs of the Church*
ca. 1450
Oil on panel
This panel is assumed to be the left one of a triptych. The princes and martyrs are crowded together in the foreground, each holding his appropriate attributes.

19th-c. Gallery   MADAME ADELAIDE LABILLE-GUIARD   *Mme Adelaide of France*
French, 1749–1803   ca. 1787
Oil on canvas
Although this is a full-length portrait, Labille-Guiard is best known for her miniature portraits. Both she and her husband painted for the Russian court.

19th-c. Gallery   JEAN LEON GEROME   *Pollice Verso*
French, 1824–1904   1874
Oil on canvas
Gérôme was a painter of the Romantic period and very popular with the wealthy French middle class. He painted mostly historical and mythological scenes.

Western Gallery   JOHN MIX STANLEY   *Chain of Spires Along the Gila River*
American, 1814–1872   1855
Oil on canvas
Well known for his paintings and drawings of Indians, Stanley painted this view while accompanying the Kearny expedition through Arizona.

American Gallery   EASTMAN JOHNSON   *Portrait of Clara Hall*
American, 1824–1906   1873
Oil on panel
Johnson is best known for his paintings of American domestic life. The strength and realism of his work is derived from his early studies in Düsseldorf and from Dutch genre scenes.

Contemporary Gallery   JOSEPH STELLA   *Flowers*
Italian/American, 1877–1946   1931
Oil on canvas
Known as the first American Futurist, Stella anticipated the abstract art of the 1950s and 1960s. This vividly colored fantasy features flowers of architectural shape in the background.

Exterior view. Courtesy Phoenix Art Museum, Phoenix

FACILITIES

Tours, Lectures and *Audiovisual Presentations* are sponsored by the museum. Call for further information.

Temporary Exhibitions culled from the museum's collection or *Loan Exhibitions* from other institutions are regular features of the museum's program.

The *Museum Reference Library* is open to the public.

The *Museum Shop* features books, art reproductions and crafts from around the world.

Hours: Tuesday–Saturday, 10 A.M.–5 P.M.; Wednesday, 10 A.M.–9 P.M.; Sunday, 1 P.M.–5 P.M.; *Closed:* Mondays, holidays.

Admission: Free.

SUN CITY

SUN CITY/PHOENIX ART MUSEUM
9744 West Bell Rd.
Sun City, AZ 85351
Tel: (602)974-2583

This is a branch of the Phoenix Art Museum, featuring monthly changing exhibitions from the museum's permanent collection and from touring exhibitions. Lectures, musicales, and films are all part of the regular programming.

FACILITIES

Hours: *Open September through May:* Tuesday–Saturday, 10 A.M.–4 P.M.; Sundays, 1 P.M.–4 P.M. *Closed:* Mondays.

Admission: Free.

TEMPE

UNIVERSITY ART COLLECTIONS
ARIZONA STATE UNIVERSITY
2nd Floor, Matthews Center
Tempe, AZ 85281
Tel: (602)965-2874

This university collection is housed in three galleries. Its first benefactor was
Oliver B. James, who bequeathed it his American art collection of 18th- to
20th-century works.

SAMPLING THE COLLECTION

19th-c. **American** **Gallery**	ALBERT PINKHAM RYDER American, 1847–1917	*The Canal* ca. 1915 Oil on canvas

Ryder's tremendous grasp of volume, space and design, so vividly expressed
in *The Canal,* enhanced the transcendental and sometimes ominous mood that
became a dominant quality in his developed monumental style.

19th-c. **American** **Gallery**	HIRAM POWERS American, 1805–1873	*George Washington* Marble

One of the first sculptured portraits of the father of our country, this is a
Neoclassical example by a very popular sculptor of his time.

19th-c. **American** **Gallery**	JOHN JAMES AUDUBON American, 1785–1851	*Osprey and the Otter and* *the Salmon* 1844 Oil on canvas

This painting has the vivid coloring and masterful technique which is found in
all of Audubon's work.

American **Primitive** **Gallery**	JOHN SCHOLL American, 1827–ca. 1916	*Solomon's Temple* ca. 1900 Wood

This Victorian primitive sculpture represents the universe and the majesty of
God. It is a major piece in the university's large collection of Americana.

Contemporary **Pottery** **Gallery**	MARIA MARTINEZ American, ca. 1881–1980	*Collection of 29* *San Ildefonso Black Pottery*

Martinez, renowned for the black-on-black style of pottery that she invented,
became interested in traditional Pueblo pottery about 1910 when asked to
duplicate a potsherd excavated from an archeological site.

FACILITIES

Guided Tours, Lectures, Films, Gallery Talks and *Concerts* are all available.
Write or call for schedule.

Temporary Exhibitions culled from the university art collections or *Loan Exhibitions* from other institutions are regular features of the university's program.

The *Sales Shop* offers handmade items from around the world, such as South

American weaving, African baskets, Japanese paper wallets, Mexican toys and contemporary posters of famous works of art.

Hours: Monday–Friday, 8 A.M.–5 P.M.; Sunday, 1 P.M.–5 P.M.. *Closed:* Saturdays, federal and state holidays.

Admission: Free.

TUCSON

MUSEUM OF ART
Speedway at Olive
University of Arizona
Tucson, AZ 85721
Tel: (602)626-1180

This university art collection includes works from 6th-century China through the contemporary American scene. Its special strength lies in the C. Leonard Pfeiffer Collection of American painting, which consists of approximately 100 works of the 1930s, 40s and 50s; the Samuel H. Kress Collection of Italian art and the Gallagher Memorial Collection of contemporary American and European painting and sculpture.

SAMPLING THE COLLECTION

C. LEONARD PFEIFFER COLLECTION   **2nd Floor**

EDWARD HOPPER   *The City*
American, 1882–1967   Oil
Hopper's work is marked by a feeling of isolation. His anonymous figures and the way in which he employs light and shadow on his architectural and geometric forms serve to heighten this quality.

REGINALD MARSH   *Monday Night at the*
American, 1898–1954   *Metropolitan*
                                     1939
                                     Tempera and oil
Marsh commenced his career as an illustrator and this training made him more sensitive to design than to color. His subject matter was generally concerned with city life, frequently in its more sleazy aspects.

STUART DAVIS   *Industry*
American, 1894–1964   1942
                                     Oil
Urban life with its color, noise and tempo provided Stuart with his subject matter. His work was influenced by the Fauvists and Cubists.

MARC CHAGALL   *Winter in Moscow*
Russian, b. 1887   Crayon and pencil
Chagall's paintings are filled with poetry and fantasy and make special use of rich colors. His work has evolved from Cubism to representational Expressionism and is strongly influenced by his Russian-Jewish origins.

2nd Floor   *SAMUEL H. KRESS COLLECTION*

FERNANDO GALLEGO   *Retablo Panels*
Spanish, ca. 1443–ca. 1508   15th c.
This series of altar panels done in the Hispano-Flemish style, survived the
Peninsula Wars. They illustrate biblical stories from the Creation to the Last
Judgment.

TINTORETTO (JACOPO ROBUSTI)   *Venus Lamenting the Death*
Italian, Venetian, 1518–1594   *of Adonis*
                                 1576–1582
                                 Oil
Bent on gaining fame and fortune, Tintoretto employed a large workshop and
much of his work survives today. He endeavored to synthesize Michelangelo's
drawing with Titian's color.

GIOVANNI BATTISTA TIEPOLO   *Circumcision of the Children*
Italian, 1696–1770   *of Israel*
                                 1735–1745
Tiepolo, the foremost Italian Rococo painter, decorated scores of churches and
palaces. This painting was executed when he was working in a lighter and freer
style.

MARIE LOUISE ELIZABETH
VIGEE-LEBRUN   *The Countess of Schoenfeld*
French, 1755–1842   1793
Court painter to Marie Antoinette, Vigée-Lebrun painted mostly women and
children in a decorative style. She survived the Revolution and became popular
in many European courts.

2nd Floor   *GALLAGHER MEMORIAL COLLECTION*

JEAN (HANS) ARP   *La Venus Meudon*
Alsatian/French, 1887–1966   Bronze
Arp was one of the original Dadaists. His organic sculptures with their polished
finishes and sensuous curves often have sexual motifs.

ALEXANDER CALDER   *Blue Moon over the Steeple*
American, 1898–1976   1965
                                 Painted metal
Calder was the originator of mobiles, sculptures concerned with the relationship
of objects in space. The first were manually or motor-driven. Later ones moved
more naturally by wind.

MARK ROTHKO   *Green on Blue*
American, 1903–1970   1956
                                 Oil
Rothko's paintings are usually large and abstract and have rectangular bands of
color with soft edges. He was an Abstract Expressionist.

MORRIS LOUIS   *Number IV*
American, 1912–1962   1957
                                 Oil
Louis's characteristic paintings are large with bright, clear colors applied without
detectable brush strokes. The overlapping vertical veils of color are stained onto
unsized canvas.

FACILITIES

Guided Tours are available by trained guides.

Changing Exhibitions are regularly featured.

Posters and *Publications* on the collections and exhibitions are for sale.

Hours: Monday–Saturday, 9 A.M.–5 P.M.; Sunday, 12 P.M.–5 P.M.; *Closed:* New Year's, July 4, Thanksgiving, Christmas.

Admission: Free.

TUCSON MUSEUM OF ART
140 North Main
Tucson, AZ 85705
Tel: (602)624-2333

Located in its new quarters since 1975, the museum lies within El Presidio Historic District. History and geography bind southern Arizona to Mexico and Latin America in their cultural heritage. The permanent collections of pre-Columbian, Spanish Colonial and more recent works reflect this melding of peoples.

SAMPLING THE COLLECTION

PRE-COLUMBIAN ART

Palmate Stone
A.D. 600–900
Carved volcanic stone

This vertical, egg-shaped stone resembles a palm frond. It is covered with a low relief of a human form. The palmate stones were possibly designed to fit the center of the yoke below.

Ceremonial Yoke Fragment
A.D. 800
Carved stone

This enigmatic yoke is carved in a curvilinear style.

MEXICAN   *Stela*
Central Veracruz, Classic Period,   A.D. 800
Totanac Culture   Carved stone

This stela, carved with a bearded standing figure, is typical of the sculpture of the period carved in low relief depicting gods and humans.

PERUVIAN   *Textile Fragment*
Ica Valley, Late Nazca Culture   A.D. 800–1000
                                 Dyed cameloid fiber (vicuna)

This fragment symbolized the puma's (cat or jaguar) power and strength in geometric patterns, a type of decoration common to the textiles and ceramics of the period.

PERUVIAN   *Ceremonial Poncho*
Central or South Coast, Classic   A.D. 800–1100
Tiahuanaco Style   Cotton and wool

Ramps, Lower Gallery and Exhibition Galleries. *Courtesy Tucson Museum of Art, Tucson*

This poncho represents the puma's head, back and tail. The puma, along with the human head, the condor, stars, fish, the winged eye and a stepped pattern, were common themes of the period.

SPANISH COLONIAL ART

SPANISH

Chest
ca. 19th c.
Wood, ivory inlay, iron fittings

This chest belonged to Archduke Maximilian, Emperor of Mexico (1864–1867). Repetitive decorative designs inlaid in ivory reveal influences of the Mudejar, a combination of Christian and Mohammedan styles evolved in Spain in the Middle Ages.

PERUVIAN
Cuzco

Journey of the Magi
ca. 1550–1650
Wood, paper, polychrome, glass, fiber, gesso

Youth, middle age and old age are each represented by a wise man: youth by a black wise man on a gray elephant, middle age on a brown camel and old age on an ochre horse.

SPANISH
Hispano-Flemish Style

Slaughter of the Innocents
ca. 1470–1485
Oil on gessoed oak panel with gold leaf in the brocade in the center.

In style, this painting reveals the influence of Fernando Gallego and/or his atelier. He was the leading Master of this style and was influential throughout Castile.

CONTEMPORARY MEXICAN ART

JOSE LUIS CUEVAS
Mexican, b. 1933

Homage to Zuevedo
1969
14 color lithographs
portfolio 9 in a limited edition of 25

Cuevas is a self-taught painter and illustrator whose original, intense pictures are concerned with social injustice.

18TH-, 19TH- AND 20TH-CENTURY AMERICAN AND EUROPEAN ART

MARSDEN HARTLEY
American, 1877–1943

Aix Landscape
1926
Oil on canvas

This painting with its broad strokes and raw primary colors is in post-Cézanne style. In his last years, Hartley painted mostly landscapes, returning to representational expression.

JACQUES LIPCHITZ
Lithuanian/American, 1891–1973

Flight
1940
Bronze

This Cubistic work is in Baroque curvilinear style. Lipchitz associated this biblical theme—the Israelite flight from bondage—with the oppressed people in Eastern European countries during World War II.

MARINO MARINI
Italian, 1901–1980

Horse and Rider
1948
Bronze

Marini's early *Horse and Rider* symbolized hope and gratitude. This later piece shows his slow transition into an Expressionistic stance of pessimism and fear of the character of man and his world.

GERMAN

Our Lady of the Immaculate Conception
late 18th c.
European pine, polychrome, lace, glass

This figure represents the descent of the Holy Spirit upon Mary, depicting her in a state of purity while three carved angel heads suspend her above the realm of the world.

FACILITIES

Guided Tours by guides are available on 48-hours' notice.

Temporary Exhibitions culled from the museum's collection or *Loan Exhibitions* from other institutions are regular features of the museum's program.

Lectures are offered. Call for information.

The *Sales Gallery* offers crafts and fine arts by Arizona artists. Magazines, catalogs, cards and art wrapping paper are also sold. The most popular items are contemporary ceramics, jewelry and textiles with prices ranging from $19 to $1,000.

The *Craft Gallery* sells selected works by professional craftsmen of the Tucson Craft Guild.

La Casa Cordova was built about 1850, when Mexico governed the Tucson Presidio. It has been restored as a Mexican heritage museum.

Hiram Sanford Stevens Home was developed by an early merchant; he created gardens whose trees still shade the museum complex.

Washington-Meyer House, is a traditional adobe that has been, in its patchwork history, a barracks, home, garage and bail-bond office; it is currently part of the Tucson Museum of Art School.

Edward Nye Fish Home

The *Tucson Museum of Art Library* contains general art reference material with special emphasis on ethnic arts. It is contained in the former home of a prominent citizen. Located at 119 N. Main Ave., Tel: (602)623-4881, it is open Monday–Friday, 10 A.M.–3 P.M..

Hours: Tuesday–Saturday, 10 A.M.–5 P.M.; Sunday, 1 P.M.–5 P.M.. *Closed:* Mondays, major holidays.

Admission: Free.

WINDOW ROCK

NAVAJO TRIBAL MUSEUM
P.O. Box 308
Window Rock, AZ 86515
Tel: (602)871-4941, ext. 1457 or 1459

The Navajo Tribal Museum was established in 1961 to collect and preserve for the Navajo people, themselves, material relating to their own history and culture and to the natural history of their homeland. Vast quantities of such material have been removed from Navajoland over the years, both by private individuals and other museums. Fortunately, some of this material is now beginning slowly to find its way back home, the result of concerned individuals who recognize the importance of a people retaining their own culture. Descendants of early reservation traders frequently contact the museum concerning the donation of material gathered by their grandparents in the 1800s and early 1900s. The museum's collections now number approximately 7,000 items, including excellent examples of Navajo weaving from the mid-1800s to the present, all styles of handmade Navajo jewelry, religious and ethnographic material, a sizable collection of prehistoric and contemporary pottery, and representative works of Navajo and other Southwest artists. Permanent exhibits tell the story of Navajo history and culture and of the prehistory of the region. Temporary exhibits are installed periodically for a broader interpretive program.

FACILITIES

Separate from the building are a *Library,* containing reference material on Navajos and other Indians, and a *Zoo,* housing animals native to the area.

Hours: *April–November:* Monday–Saturday, 9 A.M.–5 P.M.; Sunday, 1 P.M. – 5 P.M. *December–March:* Monday–Friday, 9 A.M.–5 P.M. *Closed:* National and tribal holidays.

Admission: Free.

CALIFORNIA

BERKELEY

JUDAH L. MAGNES MEMORIAL MUSEUM
2911 Russell St.
Berkeley, CA 94705
Tel: (415)849-2710

The museum, established in 1962, is located in a historic mansion on one-half acre of landscaped ground enhanced by a sculpture garden. It houses a collection of Jewish ceremonial objects and fine arts that include illuminated Hebrew marriage certificates, Hanukkah lamps and 19th-century genre paintings of Jewish life. Additionally, there is a Yemenite craftsman's workshop. The museum maintains six Jewish cemeteries of the gold-rush period.

SAMPLING THE COLLECTION

DUTCH   *Hanukkah Lamp*
                                   18th c.
                                   Brass

The Hanukkah lamp commemorates the rededication of the temple after the Maccabean victory over the Syrians in 165 B.C. Hanukkah is marked by lighting each of eight lights on successive days.

Dutch Hanukkah Lamp. *Courtesy Judah L. Magnes Memorial Museum, Berkeley*

13

GERMAN   *Torah Ark Curtain*
                                              18th c.
                                              Brocade
The Torah scroll, the most sacred object in the synagogue, contains the first five books of the Bible. A richly ornamented curtain embroidered in all-over pattern with Hebrew inscriptions usually hangs before the ark housing it.

FACILITIES

Lectures by visiting artists and scholars are presented and there are regular Monday-at-Magnes morning lectures.

Changing Exhibitions of the work of a variety of artists is a regular museum feature.

The *Goldstein Library* is available for reference and contains rare books and manuscripts.

The *Western Jewish History Center* caters to those interested in researching Jewish family or community history in the eleven Western states.

The *Gift Shop* carries handcrafted Jewish ceremonial art and jewelry by Bay Area craftspeople in silver, brass and ceramics. Prices range from $10 to $300. Publications and catalogs of the museum range from $2 to $15.

Hours: Sunday–Friday, 10 A.M.–4 P.M. *Closed:* Saturdays, Jewish holidays.

Admission: Free.

UNIVERSITY ART MUSEUM, BERKELEY
2626 Bancroft Way
Berkeley, CA 94720
Tel: (415)642-0808

In 1963, it was recommended that an art museum be added to the Berkeley campus. At the same time a gift by Hans Hofmann of 45 of his paintings with funds to build a gallery to house them provided the impetus for this striking building. The architects, Richard L. Jorasch, Ronald E. Wagner and Mario Ciampi were selected in a national competition which resulted, in 1970, in the largest university art building in the world, with a radical design that works. The permanent collection houses artworks from almost all countries and historical periods, but its most extensive holdings are in 20th-century American painting. There is also an excellent and rapidly growing collection of Asian art.

SAMPLING THE COLLECTION

Gallery 2   *ORIENTAL COLLECTION*

SAKAI HOITSU   *The Poet Hitomaro*
Japanese, 1761–1828   Hanging scroll, ink and color on silk
Hoitsu was considered the greatest painter of his day. He was a more Rococo artist than his predecessors but brought more realism to his work.

Interior view. Courtesy University Art Museum, Berkeley

TAO CHI   *Reminiscences of Nanking*   **Gallery 2**
Chinese, 1641–before 1720   1704
                                     Ink and light color on paper
Tao Chi was an important individualist painter of the Ch'ing Dynasty. This
10-leaf album exemplifies his original and daring style. Vigorous brushwork and
opulent color were tempered by discrimination and attention to detail.

KUSHIRO UNSEN   *Landscape with Man and Crane*   **Gallery 2**
Japanese, 1759–1811   *Approaching Pavilion*
                                     1793
                                     Hanging scroll, ink and light colors
                                     on silk
This was a period in which Japanese painters turned from stylization and strove
for greater naturalism in their work.

CH'EN HUNG-SHOU   *A Scholar Instructing Women*   **Gallery 2**
Chinese, 1599–1652   *in the Arts*
                                     Hanging scroll, ink and light colors
                                     on silk
The paintings of the Ming Dynasty were intricate, abundantly detailed and
dignified.

ATT. TO LO CHUANG   *The Zen Poet Han Shan*   **Gallery 2**
Chinese, 13th c.   Hanging scroll, ink on paper

Sung Dynasty painting is divided into five categories. This work is from the last period. It was known as the "spontaneous style" and flourished particularly in the monasteries of South China.

Gallery 4   *20TH-CENTURY PAINTING AND SCULPTURE*

FRANCIS BACON	*Lying Figure with Hypodermic*
British, b. 1910	*Syringe*
	1963
	Oil on canvas

Bacon's controversial paintings are addressed to our feelings. His work is rooted in reality but his eerie, horrible, often screaming subjects exert an existential grip on us.

HELEN FRANKENTHALER	*Before the Caves*
American, b. 1928	1958
	Oil on canvas

Frankenthaler's original technique of saturating unprimed, unsized canvas with thin pigment is attributable to the influence of Jackson Pollock. Her paintings are usually very large.

MARK ROTHKO	*Number 207 (Red over Dark*
American, 1903–1970	*Blue on Dark Gray)*
	1961
	Oil on canvas

Rothko's early work was influenced by the Surrealists, but he is best known for his large abstract paintings whose horizontal bands of pigment have blurred edges.

DAVID SMITH	*Voltri XIII*
American, 1906–1965	1962
	Steel

Smith's first steel sculptures were of found objects. He later turned to "space drawings," lighter, more open works comparable to calligraphy in space.

Gallery 6   *HANS HOFMANN COLLECTION*

Hofmann (German/American, 1880–1966), an influential teacher, was first attracted to Cubism and Fauvism. In the 1950s he became a leading Abstract Expressionist, dribbling and splotching strong colors in works of great vitality. The museum contains the world's largest collection of Hofmann paintings.

FACILITIES

Guided Tours, Lectures and *Gallery Talks* are available.

Temporary Exhibitions culled from the museum's collection or *Loan Exhibitions* from other institutions are regular features of the museum's program.

The *Pacific Film Archive* of the museum presents nightly public showings of films in the theater.

The *Swallow Restaurant* offers gourmet sandwiches and desserts.

The *Bookstore* contains books on art, film, crafts and children's books. It also sells distinctive handcrafted jewelry, scarves and other accessories. Prices range from 50¢ to over $100.

Hours: Wednesday–Sunday, 11 A.M.–5 P.M. *Closed:* Mondays, Tuesdays, New Year's, Christmas.

Admission: Free.

BEVERLY HILLS

FRANCIS E. FOWLER, JR., FOUNDATION MUSEUM
9215 Wilshire Blvd.
Beverly Hills, CA 90210
Tel: (213)278-8010

Assembled by Mr. Fowler over a period of 50 years, the museum's collections consist of decorative arts of European and Asiatic origin and English, Early American and continental silver dating from the 15th to the 19th century.

SAMPLING THE COLLECTION

THOMAS BAMPTON
English, 16th c.

12 Plates
1567
Parcel-gilt silver

A fine example of engraved work.

GERMAN

2 Drinking Cups
late 15th and mid-16th c.
Silver-mounted leather

Both cups are in the form of a shoe. The mount of the earlier one is engraved with the arms of the city of Memmingen, the later one with a man and spear about to attack a lion.

GERMAN

Drinking Cup
17th c.
Gilt silver

This cup, in the shape of a rampant bull, was made in Lüneburg in the early part of the century.

JURGEN RICHELS
German, ?–1711

Drinking Cup
late 17th c.
Gilt silver

This large cup was made in Hamburg and is in the form of a rampant lion.

PAUL DE LAMERIE
British, 1688–1751

Ewer and Basin
1726
Gilt silver

De Lamerie, the most renowned silversmith in English history, achieved world-wide fame. He brought new forms of decoration to his craft. This work bears the arms of George Anson, 1st Baron of Litchfield.

ROBERT CALDERWOOD
Irish, 16th c.

Wine Fountain
1754
Silver

This large piece is an outstanding survivor of Irish Georgian work and bears a Dublin hallmark.

FACILITIES

Hours: Monday–Saturday, 1 P.M.–5 P.M. *Closed:* Sundays, holidays.
Admission: Free.

CHERRY VALLEY

EDWARD-DEAN MUSEUM OF DECORATIVE ART
9401 Oak Glen Rd.
Cherry Valley, CA 92223
Tel: (714)845-2626

The atmosphere of an 18th-century home prevails as one enters the museum of eight spacious rooms set amid 16 landscaped acres. The collection consists primarily of European decorative arts; furniture; paintings; tapestries and porcelains. Sculpture dating from the 3rd century B.C. and a selection of Oriental pieces are also to be viewed.

SAMPLING THE COLLECTION

KARL HANS BERNEVITZ   *Icarus*
German, 1858–?   1903
                             Bronze
This sculpture once belonged to Hermann Goering. Other of Bernevitz's works can be seen in Latvia and Germany.

DAVID ROBERTS   *Watercolors*
British, 1796–1864   1820–1850
Roberts, once a house painter, had no formal training. His reputation was based on his ability as an architectural draftsman who gave careful attention to details of buildings in his paintings.

Pine Room   GRINLING GIBBONS   *Paneling*
British, 1648–1721   17th c.
                             Pine
Gibbons, the most sought-after carver of his time, specialized in flora and fauna observed directly from nature. He embellished the rooms of large country homes such as this state bedroom of the Earl of Essex at Cassiobury Park.

Blue Room   JOHN BROADWOOD   *Pianoforte*
British, 1732–1812   1804
Broadwood reconstructed the square piano, inventing the soft and sustaining pedals and making other improvements. This example is one of 6 extant of the 16 he made that year.

FACILITIES

Guided Tours may be arranged.

Changing Exhibitions of the work of a variety of artists is a regular museum feature.

The *English Garden,* with its reflection pool, is an inviting place for visitors to stroll.

Visitors are allowed to pick fruit from the trees in season in the *Cherry Orchard.*

Museum House on Grounds   The *Art Sales Gallery and Gift Shop* feature paintings and crafts priced from $1 to $500.

Hours: Tuesday–Saturday, 10 A.M.–5 P.M.; Sunday, 1 P.M.–5 P.M. *Closed:* Mondays, national holidays, two weeks following Labor Day.

Admission: Adults, $1; senior citizens, 50¢; students, 50¢; children under 12, free.

FRESNO

FRESNO ARTS CENTER
3033 East Yale Ave.
Fresno, CA 93703
Tel: (209)485-4810

In 1914, the Fresno Art League was formed, a precursor of the Fresno Arts Center which was not incorporated until 1949. In 1960, as a result of a major fund-raising campaign, a new building was opened at its present location in Radio Park, the geographic center of Fresno. The permanent collection houses predominantly Mexican and Oriental artifacts along with Californian and Western paintings illustrating the blending of the varied cultures that were established in the Central Valley.

SAMPLING THE COLLECTION

DIEGO RIVERA
Mexican, 1886–1957

El Dia de Los Flores,
Xochimilco
1926
Oil

Rivera settled in Paris in 1911, where he was influenced by Cubism. Returning to Mexico in 1921 he developed a nationalistic style expressing his political and social concerns in monumental murals.

JOAN SAVO
American, 20th c.

Untitled
1978
Oil on canvas

Earlier in her career Savo, an area artist, painted figurative pieces but now produces nonobjective Color Field paintings.

KATCHADOR BOROIAN
Armenian, b. 1889

Untitled
1979
Needlepoint

Boroian first worked as a commercial artist. His early charcoals, oils and watercolors were influenced by Art Nouveau. Today he creates mainly batiks and needlepoint.

FACILITIES

Tours of the exhibitions are conducted by trained guides.

Lectures are presented by artists whose work is currently on exhibition.

Changing Exhibitions are mounted every four to six weeks and feature crafts, photography, paintings and drawings, graphics and sculpture from a wide variety of sources.

The *Rental Gallery* offers an ever-changing selection of paintings and drawings for rental or purchase. Rentals are permitted for three months. The major part of the fee may be applied to the purchase price if one decides to buy.

Bags, The Beaux Arts Gift Shop, carries a variety of items created by local artists.

Hours: Tuesday–Sunday, 10 A.M.–4:30 P.M.; Wednesday, 7:30 P.M.–10 P.M.
         Closed: Mondays.

Admission: Free.

LA JOLLA

LA JOLLA MUSEUM OF CONTEMPORARY ART
700 Prospect St.
La Jolla, CA 92037
Tel: (714)454-3541

The museum commands a stunning view of the Pacific Coast. Facilities include a sculpture garden and a 500-seat auditorium. American and European art since the 1930s dominates the collection, and the museum favors the avant-garde.

SAMPLING THE COLLECTION

RICHARD ARTSCHWAGER   *Untitled Construction*
American, b. 1924   1967
                             Formica on wood
Artschwager is an internationally known painter and sculptor.

CARL ANDRE   *36 Pieces of Zinc and*
American, b. 1935   *Magnesium*
                             1969
André is known as a Minimalist sculptor. This subtle work is a square of alternating metallic tonalities.

AGNES MARTIN   *Untitled*
Canadian, b. 1911   1962
Martin's predilection for the fine and personal expression allowed in drawing influences the character of her paintings, which are usually based on a grid structure.

ROBERT MANGOLD   *Two Squares Within a*
American, b. 1938   *Square and Two Triangles*
                             1936
                             Acrylic on canvas
Mangold is a Minimalist whose paintings are variations on geometric themes which he often arrives at by arithmetical means. He works through colors and scales in series.

AL HELD   *Untitled*
American, b. 1928   1965
                             Acrylic on canvas
A superb public example of the artist's primary color, hard-edge compositions.

FACILITIES

Luncheon Lectures are held monthly with guest lecturers speaking on a variety of art-related subjects.

Exhibitions featuring selections from the permanent collection of 20th-century art, the international design collection, and changing exhibitions of work by contemporary artists are presented in seven galleries that include over 13,000 square feet of exhibit space.

Sherwood Hall, the museum's auditorium, offers a variety of programs, including the annual Fall San Diego International Film Festival, occasional films, dramatic presentations, concerts and lectures.

The *Museum Shop* has a large assortment of jewelry, baskets, lacquerware and stationery as well as books and catalogs.

Hours: Tuesday–Friday, 10 A.M.–5 P.M.; Saturday–Sunday, 12:30 P.M.–5 P.M.
         Closed: Mondays, Thanksgiving, Christmas, New Year's.

Admission: Free.

LONG BEACH

LONG BEACH MUSEUM OF ART
2300 East Ocean Blvd.
Long Beach, CA 90803
Tel: (213)439-2119

The museum, founded in 1951, was erected in 1912, serving first as a private home. It is located on a bluff overlooking the Pacific Ocean and surrounded by significant architectural structures of Long Beach. The permanent collection specializes in 20th-century American art.

SAMPLING THE COLLECTION

GEORGE RICKEY	*Two Lines Up-Spread*	**Sculpture**
American, b. 1907	1971	**Garden**
	Stainless steel	

Rickey's kinetic sculptures, many of long metal strips, are usually outdoors, dependent on air for their motion. When stirred by breezes, they move slowly, suggestive of serenity itself.

CLAIRE FALKENSTEIN	*Structure and Flow*	**Sculpture**
American, b. 1909	1968	**Garden**
	Copper tubing and fused glass	
	The Point as a Set	
	1965	
	Welded copper fusing and tubed glass	

Executed in Falkenstein's mature style, these animated open shapes have architectural qualities, are complex yet well balanced.

Sculpture Garden	PETER VOULKOS American, b. 1924	*Untitled* 1968 Multi-metal

Voulkos, a ceramicist, abandoned traditional expressions in clay to create abstract sculptures. In 1959 he quit clay to work in metal, mostly bronze. His mature work is balanced and incisive.

Sculpture Garden	HARRY BERTOIA American, b. 1915	*Flora-Fauna* 1966 Welded bronze

Although Bertoia's work is abstract it is suggestive of natural forms. Flow welding of metal alloys covers his metal sculpture.

FACILITIES

Tours and *Lectures* are offered.

Temporary Exhibitions culled from the museum's collection or *Loan Exhibitions* from other institutions are regular features of the museum's program.

The *Carriage House Bookshop and Gallery* carries new books, limited editions and some rare books. Fine quality craft items from the Western United States are also sold.

Hours: Wednesday–Sunday, 12 P.M.–5 P.M.   *Closed:* Mondays, Tuesdays, legal holidays.

Admission: Free.

LOS ANGELES

CRAFT AND FOLK ART MUSEUM
5814 Wilshire Blvd.
Los Angeles, CA 90036
Tel: (213)937-5544

The museum, incorporated in 1973, is dedicated to the exhibition, presentation and teaching of folk art and handcrafts. A haven from synthetics and mass production, it presents artists, artisans and their crafts to the public in changing exhibitions. These exhibitions cover a wide variety of crafts and folk art, from the rapidly diminishing output of vanishing exotic cultures to the latest contemporary efforts.

The museum does have a small permanent collection that is not always on view.

FACILITIES

Lectures and *Films* are presented.

The *Museum Shop* carries a wide selection of contemporary crafts and folk art.

Hours: Tuesday–Sunday, 11 A.M.–5 P.M. Friday evening open until 8 P.M.

Admission: Free.

FREDERICK S. WIGHT ART GALLERY
UNIVERSITY OF CALIFORNIA, LOS ANGELES
405 Hilgard Ave.
Los Angeles, CA 90024
Tel: (213)825-1461

Twelve exhibitions of painting, sculpture, prints and drawings, architecture and design are presented annually in close conjunction with the (UCLA) Museum of Cultural History and the Grunwald Center for the Graphic Arts. The permanent holdings include the Franklin D. Murphy Sculpture Garden, 69 sculptures from the 20th century located in the north end of the campus.

SAMPLING THE COLLECTION

HENRI MATISSE French, 1869–1954	*La Gerbe* 1953 Gouache collage	Lobby Entrance of Wight Gallery

Matisse was a major figure of 20th-century art, a sculptor and a painter. This work was completed during his last year of life in a technique still available to him despite his infirmities.

	Bas Relief I-1909, II-1913, III-1917, IV-1930 Bronze 6/10	Murphy Sculpture Garden in the Dickson Art Center

This series, known as *The Backs,* progresses from a representative rendition of a powerful back as seen in *Bas Relief I* to the comparatively abstract execution of *Bas Relief IV.*

JEAN (HANS) ARP Alsatian/French, 1887–1966	*Pagoda Fruit* 1949 Bronze	Murphy Sculpture Garden

Early in his career, Arp exhibited with the Surrealists but soon after developed his own individual style. His organic forms are expressed in smooth, curved surfaces.

JACQUES LIPCHITZ Lithuanian/American, 1891–1973	*The Song of the Vowels* 1931–1943 Bronze 7/7	Murphy Sculpture Garden

Influenced by Cubism, Lipchitz moved on to openwork sculpture and then to biomorphic forms often of religious subjects. Here the theme, King David and the harp, incorporate Cubist understanding.

AUGUSTE RODIN French, 1840–1917	*The Walking Man* 1905 Bronze	Murphy Sculpture Garden

Rodin modeled this statue early in his career as preparation for his St. John the Baptist. Because fragmentary sculpture was not accepted at the time, acclaim was withheld until later.

HENRY MOORE British, b. 1898	*Two-Piece Reclining Figure,* *No. 3* 1960 Bronze 5/7	Murphy Sculpture Garden

In this sculpture, two islands emerge from a bronze sea. The head-and-chest piece is penetrated with one of the holes, a device Moore has utilized since the 1930s.

Murphy Sculpture Garden   GASTON LACHAISE   *Standing Woman*
French/American, 1882–1935   1932
Bronze
This is the last life-sized figure Lachaise completed before his death. Typical of the massive, unadorned female nudes he favored, it pays tribute to woman as a fertility symbol.

Murphy Sculpture Garden   BARBARA HEPWORTH   *Oval Form*
British, 1903–1975   1962–1963
Bronze 1/7
Hepworth's abstract, organic sculptures of this period are often slender, curved, connected shapes—monumental but graceful.

Murphy Sculpture Garden   ALEXANDER CALDER   *Button Flower*
American, 1898–1976   1959
Sheet steel, painted
Calder's monumental stabiles are stationary constructions that are extremely heavy in contrast to his air-propelled mobiles. His whimsical work is both mechanical and organic.

Murphy Sculpture Garden   GERHARD MARCKS   *Maja*
German, b. 1889   1941
Bronze
Marck's female figures are heavily influenced by ancient Greek and Romanesque sculpture combined with a controlled Expressionism.

Murphy Sculpture Garden   RICHARD HUNT   *Why?*
American, b. 1935   1974
Bronze 2/3
Hunt's semiabstract welded sculptures are of industrial metal and found objects. In the 1970s he turned to bronze, *Why?* being his most ambitious undertaking to date.

FACILITIES

The *Sales Shop* carries catalogs of past and present exhibitions as well as various gift items from around the world.

Hours: Tuesday–Friday, 11 A.M.–5 P.M.; Saturday–Sunday, 1 P.M.–5 P.M.
Closed: Mondays, August, September.

Admission: Free.

GRUNWALD CENTER FOR THE GRAPHIC ARTS
405 Hilgard Ave.
Los Angeles, CA 90024
Tel: (213)825-3783

The center is housed in the Dickson Art Center on the northern campus of the University of California, where it stores and displays its collection of over 25,000 prints and drawings ranging from the 15th century to the present. The German Expressionist prints are of special interest.

SAMPLING THE COLLECTION

ERNST LUDWIG KIRCHNER
German, 1880–1938

Drei Badende Frauen
1913
Woodcut, hand-colored

Hoffman and Frau
1916
Woodcut in color

Kirchner was first influenced by traditional German engravings. A feeling of the German Gothic is always present in his forceful individual style that nonetheless catches the nature of modern times.

EMIL NOLDE
German, 1867–1956

Knecht
1912
Woodcut

Dancer
1922
Etching and aquatint

Nolde's fierce, distorted pictures have a tormented quality. A sincerely religious man, he was attracted to and influenced by the mystery in primitive art. Throughout his career he remained an Expressionist.

FACILITIES

Hours: Monday–Friday, 9 A.M.–12 P.M.; 1 P.M.–5 P.M. *Call first for an appointment.*

Admission: Free.

HEBREW UNION COLLEGE SKIRBALL MUSEUM
**3077 University Mall
Los Angeles, CA 90007
Tel: (213)749-3424**

The museum houses a collection of biblical archeological treasures and Judaic ceremonial art reflecting the growth of Jewish civilization from early Palestine to more recent times.

SAMPLING THE COLLECTION

A Walk Through the Past tells the story of Jewish history, religion and culture from the Patriarchs to modern times. This permanent exhibit places art and historical items into instructive displays.

MAURICE MAYER
French, 19th c.

Omer Calendar
Silver and alloy, semiprecious
stones, wood, parchment, paint,
glass, enamel

Mayer was goldsmith by appointment to Napoleon III. This calendar served to count the days between Passover and the Festival of Shavuot/Weeks.

MESOPOTAMIAN
Babylonian Dynasty I,
1830–1531 B.C.

Letter with an Envelope
Terracotta

**Across from
the Egyptian
Display**

This unbaked envelope is partly broken away from the cuneiform letter underneath with its Sumerian inscription.

Settlement   PALESTINIAN   *Astarte Figurine*
in Canaan   Iron II Period, 900–586 B.C.   Terracotta
Era   This pillar-shaped body with fully architectural facial features and stylized hair and dress has a pronounced breast supported by its hands.

Coin Case   JUDEAN AND ROMAN   *Ancient Coins*
near Qumran Hasmonean Period, 1st War   Silver and bronze
Jar   Against Rome, Bar Kokhba Period,
                 2nd c. B.C.–2nd c. A.D.
                 The coins of these three periods are of various sizes and have various inscriptions.

On the Bima PALESTINIAN   *Torah Case (Tik)*
                 Nablus (Schechem)   1756
                                                          Silver, repoussé and chased, coral
                                                          and semiprecious stones
                 This elaborately ornamented case was used to hold the scroll that contained the Jewish scriptures. It was used in a synagogue for liturgical purposes.

FACILITIES

Guided Tours for individuals are available Sundays, Tuesdays, 1:30 P.M.

Recorded Tours of the permanent installation, *A Walk Through the Past,* are available: $1 per person; $1.50 for two, $4 for speaker unit appropriate for groups.

Temporary Exhibitions culled from the museum's collection or *Loan Exhibitions* from other institutions are regular features of the museum's programs.

Lectures, Films, Gallery Talks are offered. Call for information.

A *Lending Slide Library* with documentary slides on the museum's collection and related material in other collections is available.

The *Museum Shop's* merchandise runs the gamut from inexpensive greeting cards, postcards and posters selling under $1 to costly antiquities for several hundred dollars. Priced in between in the $10–$30 range is Israeli folk art, books on Jewish history and art, Israeli and Yemenite jewelry and ceremonial objects.

Hours: Tuesday–Friday, 11 A.M.–4 P.M.; Sunday, 10 A.M.–5 P.M. *Closed:* Mondays, Saturdays, national and Jewish holidays.

Admission: Free.

LOS ANGELES COUNTY MUSEUM OF ART
5905 Wilshire Blvd.
Los Angeles, CA 90036
Tel: (213)937-4250

The museum is composed of three buildings around a central sculpture plaza. It is one of the most exciting museums in this country and is host to over 1,500,000 visitors a year. The permanent collections, in the Ahmanson Gallery, range from prehistoric times to the present. The collection of Indian art is one of the best in the Western world. The holdings in Nepalese, Tibetan and Islamic art and Peruvian textiles have few equals in American museums.

Auguste Rodin, Monument to Balzac. *Courtesy Los Angeles County Museum of Art, Los Angeles, Permanent Loan of B. G. Cantor*

SAMPLING THE COLLECTION

FRA BARTOLOMMEO (BACCIO **Plaza**
DELLA PORTA) *Holy Family* **Level**
Italian, 1472–1517 Oil on canvas
Distinguished from the traditional *Holy Family* by its off-center composition, tall rectangular forms and use of canvas, this painting was probably used as a processional banner. Fra Bartolommeo brought the High Renaissance style in Florence to its fruition.

FRANS HALS *Portrait of Pieter Tjarck* **Plaza**
Dutch, ca. 1581–1666 1635–1638 **Level**
Oil on canvas
The sitter's rose, always emblematic of earthly love, suggests a wedding portrait. This, one of Hals's most classic canvases, shows more restraint and a concern with form than did his earlier work.

PAOLO CALIARI VERONESE *Allegory of Navigation* **Plaza**
Italian, Venetian, 1528–1588 (holding cross-staff) **Level**
Oil on canvas

Allegory of Navigation **Ahmanson**
(holding astrolabe) **Gallery**
Oil on canvas

These finely preserved paintings are among the most monumental of Veronese's works, usually full of architectural details and attractive people. They probably formed part of a grand decorative scheme of figures united by painted architecture.

Ahmanson Gallery, 1st Level	JAPANESE Late Heian Period, 12th c.	*Jizo Bosatsu* Carved kaya wood

Jizo, a deity depicted as a monk with shaven head, has no adornment save a jewel symbolizing power. During the Heian period, Japanese culture freed itself from continental influences culminating in the gentle, graceful Japanese style.

Ahmanson Gallery, 1st Level	CHINESE Late Chou Dynasty, 1st quarter 5th c. B.C.	*Covered Ting (tripod cauldron)* Bronze

Anarchy and constant warfare plagued the Eastern Chou period, yet bronzes were produced that are still unequaled. They were used in ceremonies to mark important events or to grace royal tombs.

Ahmanson Gallery, 1st Level	TURKISH Isnik, 1550–1560	*Dish with Lobed Rim and Flaring Body* Ceramic

This dish's overall asymmetrical and windblown design represents the second phase of ceramic tradition under the Ottoman Turks, displaying a wider palette of brilliant colors than the porcelains modeled after the Chinese Ming.

Ahmanson Gallery, 1st Level	CHINESE T'ang Dynasty, A.D. 618–906	*Horse* early 8th c. Buff white earthenware with brown, green and straw-colored glazes

The Heeramaneck horse, an example of T'ang mortuary art, is a marvel of observed naturalism in its well-balanced proportions and clarity of form. The art of polychrome glazing (san ts'ai) was a major technical achievement.

Ahmanson Gallery, 1st Level	ASSYRIAN Kalah	*Palace Reliefs of Ashurnasirpal II* 9th c. B.C. Gypseous alabaster

These five panels are probably from an antechamber for the throne hall and the "living room" of the king's apartment. The Assyrians used stone panels in royal buildings carved in high and low relief and generally painted.

Ahmanson Gallery, 3rd Level	FRANK STELLA American, b. 1936	*Protractor Variation* 1969 Fluorescent-alkyd on canvas

The *Protractor* series, begun in 1967, are based on the curvilinear, sectional shapes inherent in the geometric instrument.

Ahmanson Gallery, 3rd Level	RICHARD DIEBENKORN American, b. 1922	*Ocean Park Series #49* 1972 Oil on canvas

This series marked Diebenkorn's return to Abstract Art from over a decade of figurative work. These works deal with spatiality and the relationships between color, lateral, flat and illusionistic space, and depth.

Ahmanson Gallery, 3rd Level	MARK ROTHKO American, 1903–1970	*White Center* 1967 Oil on canvas

This is a prime work of Rothko's mature abstract style in which soft-edged rectangles of glowing atmospheric color are symmetrically arranged.

Ahmanson Gallery, 3rd Level	PABLO PICASSO Spanish, 1881–1973	*Portrait of Sebastian Juner Vidal* 1903 Oil on canvas

The subject was a painter and close friend of Picasso's during his Barcelona years. Picasso's somewhat romantic view of his friend, and probably of himself at the time, is implicit in the rather theatrical depiction. Yet the simplicity and directness make the characterization unsentimental.

HENRI MATISSE French, 1869–1954	*Heads of Jeannette* 1910–1913 Bronze	**Ahmanson Gallery, 3rd Level**

These are among the most important sculptural holdings of the museum. Matisse worked in sculpture to clarify issues in his painting. The *Heads* progress from the original life-size naturalistic conception to the abstract fifth version.

JOHN SINGLETON COPLEY American, 1738–1815	*Portrait of Hugh Montgomerie, 12th Earl of Eglinton* 1780 Oil on canvas	**Ahmanson Gallery, American Art Galleries, 3rd Level**

In 1775, Copley, the greatest American portrait painter of his time, settled in London. Montgomerie's stance as a modern Apollo Belvedere is Copley's concession to the grand manner portrait in vogue at the time.

GILBERT STUART American, 1755–1828	*Portrait of George Washington* 1822 Oil on canvas	**Ahmanson Gallery, American Art Galleries, 3rd Level**

Stuart painted Washington from life three times. From these prototypes he painted over 100 variants. This full-length portrait was known as the Lansdowne type and derived from the Athenaeum bust.

THOMAS COLE American, 1801–1848	*L'Allegro* 1845 Oil on canvas	**Ahmanson Gallery, American Art Galleries, 3rd Level**

Cole, a leader in the Hudson River School of painting, later worked "on serious compositions" of a single theme in complementary opposites. *L'Allegro* depicts the joys and *Il Penseroso,* its lost companion, the sorrows of human experience.

INDIAN Tamilnadu	*Shiva, the Lord of Dance* (Naṭarāja) ca. 10th c. Bronze with green patina	**Ahmanson Gallery, 4th Level**

Indian sculpture mirrors the postures and gestures of the dancer. Some images of dancing Naṭarājas are impressive for their size, or grace or liveliness but few are characterized by such compelling majesty as this example.

INDIAN Madhya Pradesh Sanchi	*Sālabhāñjikā (Tree Dryads)* A.D. 10–25 Sandstone	**Ahmanson Gallery, 4th Level**

This relief is from one of the oldest Buddhist sites in the world. The representation of the female, conceived in rounded volumes, emphasizing her fertility, remains the standard female type in Indian sculpture.

TIBETAN	*A Tathāgata Surrounded by Bodhisattvas* 13th c. Opaque watercolors on linen	**Ahmanson Gallery, 4th Level**

One of the most monumental and earliest of Tibetan paintings. Large tankas were hung on exterior walls for public worship on festive occasions. Strict laws of symmetry governed religious icons since the Tibetan religion associates geometric perfection with cosmic order.

FACILITIES

Temporary Exhibitions culled from the museum's collection or *Loan Exhibitions* from other institutions are regular features of the museum's program.

The *Plaza Café,* an indoor-outdoor cafeteria, is open Tuesday–Saturday, 10 A.M.–4:30 P.M.; Sunday, 10 A.M.–5:30 P.M.

The *Museum Shop* has items priced from $1 to $2,000 and offers jewelry, gifts, art books, catalogs, slides, postcards and posters. Two of the most popular selections are the museum tote bag with a Peruvian textile design and the museum cookbook illustrated with works from the permanent collection.

The *Art Rental Gallery* only rents works of art to members, although the public may purchase them.

Ahmanson Gallery For free *Guided Tours* of the permanent collection, inquire at the Information Desk.

Plaza Level The *Library* has 50,000 volumes available for adult use.

Bing Center The *Bing Theater* presents concerts, lectures and other events. It has a stimulating film program offering retrospectives, foreign, avant-garde and children's movies. Admission for most performances is $2.50 for adults. Members, children and students are charged less.

Parking is free of charge in the Hancock Park lot off Curzon Avenue, a block east of the museum.

Hours: Tuesday–Friday, 10 A.M–5 P.M.; Saturday–Sunday, 10 A.M.–6 P.M. *Closed:* Mondays, Thanksgiving, Christmas.

Admission: Free, except to special exhibitions on the Plaza Level of the Frances and Armand Hammer Wing, for which adults pay $1, children under 18 and senior citizens, 50¢.

UNIVERSITY GALLERIES, UNIVERSITY OF SOUTHERN CALIFORNIA
823 Exposition Blvd.
Los Angeles, CA 90007
Tel: (213)746-2799

The Elizabeth Holmes Fisher Gallery was established in 1939. Some 470 canvases, panels and miniatures represent the 16th to the 19th centuries in Dutch, Flemish, French, Italian, English and American painting and comprise the heart of the collection. It also contains numerous works from ancient to modern times in small sculpture, ceramics, glass, tapestry, silver, prints and drawings. Most outstanding are the 72 paintings donated by Mrs. Fisher, and the 48 Old Masters given by Dr. Armand Hammer, mainly by 16th- and 17th-century Dutch and Flemish artists. The Helen Hymer Lindhurst Gallery in the School of Architecture provides additional exhibition space. The galleries house the oldest centrally located art museum in the Los Angeles area.

SAMPLING THE COLLECTION

Hammer Collection   PETER PAUL RUBENS   *The Nativity*
Flemish, 1577–1640   Oil on canvas
Rubens was the foremost talent of the northern Baroque. He employed a large

number of assistants but most often would commence and complete a painting with his own hand.

Venus Wounded by a Thorn
Oil on canvas

This is a scene from Greek mythology although Rubens was equally adept at painting religious works, landscapes, hunting scenes and portraits.

GIOVANNI ANTONIO PELLEGRINI   *Queen Tomyris with Head*   **Hammer**
Italian, 1675–1741   *of Cyrus*   **Collection**
                                                            Oil on canvas

Pellegrini was one of the foremost Venetian decorative painters whose sprightly style anticipated that of the Tiepolos.

GERARD DOU   *Still Life with Book and Purse*   **Hammer**
Dutch, 1613–1675   Oil on panel   **Collection**

Dou, a student of Rembrandt, was a painter of carefully crafted genre scenes and portraits who used light and shadow to advantage.

MEINDERT HOBBEMA   *Holland Landscape*   **Hammer**
Dutch, 1638–1709   Oil on canvas   **Collection**

Hobbema was the last of the outstanding Dutch landscapists. He was an important influence on English landscape painters, most particularly Constable.

ASHER B. DURAND   *Kaaterskill Clove*   **Fisher**
American, 1796–1886   Oil on canvas   **Collection**

In his early years Durand was trained as an engraver. His careful style can be attributed to this background. He was a member of the Hudson River School.

GEORGE INNESS   *Storm Clouds, Berkshires*   **Fisher**
American, 1825–1894   Oil on canvas   **Collection**

Inness was mostly self-taught. His early work was akin to the Barbizon School, a group interested in the advancement of landscape painting. His later work was in sympathy with Impressionism.

WILLIAM M. HART   *Chocorua Mountain,*   **Fisher**
American, 1823–1894   *New Hampshire*   **Collection**
                                   Oil on canvas

Hart was apprenticed to a carriage-maker as a painter. He soon turned to portrait painting and then to landscapes and allegorical works.

BARTHOLOMEUS VAN DER HELST   *Portrait of a Man*   **Fisher**
Dutch, 1614–1669   **Collection**

                                   Portrait of a Woman
                                   Both oil on canvas

Helst painted both group and single portraits. He was extremely successful and a competitor of Rembrandt. His portraits were popular for their accurate likenesses.

JOHANNES (JAN) BRUEGHEL, THE   **Fisher**
ELDER   *Woodland Fair*   **Collection**
Flemish, 1568–1625   Oil on panel

Sometimes called "Velvet Brueghel" because of his interest in textiles, he was one of the leading still-life painters of this period.

BENJAMIN WEST   *Mr. John Utterson of*   **Fisher**
American, 1738–1820   *Fareham, Hampshire, England*   **Collection**
                                   Oil on canvas

West worked mostly in England, becoming court painter to George III. Many younger American painters were influenced by the realism of his portraits and historical paintings.

FACILITIES

Special Lectures are often correlated with the displays.

Temporary Exhibitions culled from the museum's collection or *Loan Exhibitions* from other institutions are regular features of the museum's program.

Hours: Monday–Friday, 12 P.M.–5 P.M. Open Saturday–Sunday, 12 P.M.–5 P.M. for special exhibitions only.

Admission: Free, except for special exhibitions, when the fee is $1.

MALIBU

J. PAUL GETTY MUSEUM
17985 Pacific Coast Highway
Malibu, CA 90265
Tel: (213)459-2306

The museum re-creates the splendor of the Villa dei Papiri, a 1st-century Roman villa, and its gardens. The original villa, located in the same region as Pompeii and Herculaneum, was buried when Vesuvius erupted in A.D. 79. The collection concentrates on three areas of interest—Greek and Roman antiquities, Renaissance and Baroque painting and French 18th-century decorative arts.

SAMPLING THE COLLECTION

Main Floor   *ANTIQUITIES*

Gallery 107, Hall of Aphrodite

Mazarin Venus
Marble
Discovered in Italy in the 16th century, this Venus was acquired by Cardinal Mazarin, minister of Louis XIV. Its prototype was the Capitoline Aphrodite. The head, breasts and right arm have been repaired.

Gallery 108, Greek Masterpieces

GREEK
Elgin Throne
carved after 300 B.C.
Marble
This throne, brought to Scotland in 1817, was probably made for a prince who freed Athens. Two very elaborate reliefs carved on either side depict earlier Greek heroes who fought for freedom.

Gallery 108, Greek Masterpieces

GREEK
The Getty Bronze
ca. 310 B.C.
The statue of an athlete victorious at Olympia may represent a Hellenistic prince from one of the dynasties established following the death of Alexander the Great. The style points to Lysippus as the sculptor.

Gallery 120, Temple of Herakles

ROMAN
Herakles Lansdowne
ca. A.D. 130
Marble
This piece was carved by a sculptor to the court of the Emperor Hadrian. It was a prototype for all other Greek heroes.

Main Peristyle Garden. *Courtesy J. Paul Getty Museum, Malibu*

REMBRANDT HARMENSZ VAN RIJN *Bust of an Old Man* **Gallery 202**
Dutch, 1606–1669 ca. 1630
  Oil on panel

  St. Bartholomew
  1661
  Oil on canvas
These two works depict the change in style that evolved during Rembrandt's long career—a transition from a bright, highly finished painting surface to one rendered in darker colors and thickly applied brush strokes.

ANTHONY VAN DYCK *Four Studies of a Negro's Head* **Gallery 203**
Flemish, 1599–1641 ca. 1617–1620
or Oil on panel
PETER PAUL RUBENS
Flemish, 1577–1640
Although the authorship of this sketch is uncertain, the model is handled with a sense of vitality not always visible in more finished works by these two artists.

GENTILE DA FABRIANO *Coronation of the Virgin* **Gallery 205**
Italian, ca. 1370–1427 early 1420s
  Tempera on panel
Originally, this panel served as a ceremonial standard in religious processions. The sumptuous garments and the lavish use of gold leaf are combined with a finely detailed rendering of the faces of Christ and Mary.

MASACCIO *St. Andrew* **Gallery 206**
Italian, Florentine, 1401–1428 1426
  Tempera on panel
St. Andrew formerly belonged to a large altarpiece painted for a church in Pisa. Influenced by Classical prototypes, Masaccio shows a new interest in the monumental and sculptural qualities of his figures.

VITTORE CARPACCIO *Hunting on the Lagoon* **Gallery 206**
Italian, Venetian, ca. 1455–1525 ca. 1490s
  Oil on panel
Carpaccio is considered to be the first great genre painter of the Italian Renaissance. This panel shows him as a careful observer of nature in his detailed treatment of the hunters, birds and boats on the lagoon.

Gallery 206   PAOLO CALIARI VERONESE   *Full-Length Portrait of a Man*
Italian, Venetian, 1528–1588   ca. 1570
Oil on canvas
Because he did not often paint portraits, this work is especially important to the
stud y of Veronese. Since the 19th century, this canvas has been referred to as
a self-portrait of the artist, but this cannot be definitely established.

Gallery 209   ANTHONY VAN DYCK   *Portrait of Agostino*
Flemish, 1599–1641   *Pallavicini*
ca. 1626
Oil on canvas
While living in Italy between 1625 and 1627, Van Dyck was often asked to
paint the nobility of this region. In the city of Genoa, Van Dyck rendered this
elegant portrait of Pallavicini, the Genoese ambassador to the papal court in
Rome.

Gallery 226   GEORGES DE LA TOUR   *The Beggars' Brawl*
French, 1593–1652   ca. 1620s
Oil on canvas
As a painter of genre scenes, La Tour is especially noted for his sense of realism.
The Beggars' Brawl is an early work showing the artist's awareness of the style
of his Dutch contemporaries.

Gallery 226   ALESSANDRO MAGNASCO   *Bacchanale*
Italian, Genoese, 1667–1749   ca. 1712
Oil on canvas
In the early part of his career, while he was active in Milan, Magnasco painted
this bacchanal scene. It was conceived in the rapid and painterly style that is
associated with this artist.

DECORATIVE ARTS

Gallery 210   ATT. TO ANDRE-CHARLES BOULLE   *Oval-Faced Pedestal Clock*
French, 1642–1732   ca. 1720
Veneered with tortoiseshell brass,
set with gilt bronze mounts
Three other pedestal clocks of this type are known to exist today. The corners
of the clock are set with male terms representing the four known continents at
the time: Africa, Europe, Asia and the Americas.

Gallery 210   JACQUES DUBOIS   *Corner Cabinet*
French, 1693–1763   ca. 1735–1740
Veneered with kingwood and *satine
rouge,* set with gilt bronze mounts
This magnificent corner cabinet is one of the monuments of French Rococo
cabinetmaking. A preliminary drawing for it exists in the Musée des Arts Deco-
ratifs in Paris and is attributed to Nicolas Pineau (1684–1754). The clock is by
Étienne Le Noir (1698–c. 1778). Rather than for a royal client with more sober
taste, Dubois was probably working this case for a rich financier. The cabinet
once belonged to members of the Viennese branch of the Rothschilds, Barons
Nathaniel and Alphonse.

Gallery 210   FRENCH   *Cabinet-on-Stand*
ca. 1675
The cabinet was made at the Gobelins Manufactory outside Paris. It is supported by two figures: Hercules on the right and his consort, Omphale, on the
left. The cabinet is veneered with a variety of exotic woods, pewter, brass,

tortoiseshell, horn and ivory, and set with gilt bronze mounts. On the central marquetry door panel is represented the cockerel of France standing supreme over the lien of the Netherlands and the eagle of the Austrian Empire, commemorating France's military victories of the 1670s.

FRENCH *Model for a Clock* **Gallery 212**
ca. 1700
Terracotta, enameled plaques
When an important object was commissioned from an artisan, it was sometimes the custom to first present the client with a working model. This is a rare instance of a full-size terracotta model for a clock that has survived surprisingly intact.

BERNARD VAN RISENBURGH *Double Desk* **Gallery 213**
French, ?–1767 ca. 1740
Veneered with tulipwood and
kingwood, with gilt bronze mounts
The double desk is the masterpiece of Bernard van Risenburgh, the most notable cabinetmaker of the Rococo period. It is traditionally believed that the desk was made for the twin daughters of Louis XV, although no documentary evidence exists to prove this.

ATT. TO JEAN HENRI RIESENER *Secretaire* **Gallery 217**
French, 1734–1806 ca. 1785
Veneered with ebony and inset with
Japane se lacquer panels, set with
gilt bronze mounts
Riesener was royal cabinetmaker to Louis XVI from 1774 to 1784. The central relief, "The Sacrifice to Cupid," is probably after a design by the sculptor Clodion. The piece was at Hamilton Palace in the 19th-century and also once formed part of the collection of Cornelius Vanderbilt.

AFTER DESIGNS BY FRANCOIS **Gallery 220**
BOUCHER *Set of Four French*
French, 1703–1770 *(Gobelins) Tapestries*
ca. 1776–1778
Ordered by Louis XVI for the Grand Duke Paul Petrovich, later Czar Paul I. The tapestries hung at the Palace of Pavlovsk near Leningrad until the Russian Revolution.

ATT. TO PIERRE GOUTHIERE *Mounted Vase* **Gallery 220**
French, 1732–ca. 1812 ca. 1780
Chinese porcelain with French gilt
bronze mounts
Two other mounted vases of this type are known to exist today, including one in the British royal collection. The vase is believed to have been purchased at the Revolutionary sale of the contents of Versailles by the Polish Countess Isabella Lubomirska, friend of Marie Antoinette.

FACILITIES

A *Tour* is provided by a 45-minute radio cassette that may be rented from the bookstore for a nominal fee.

Lectures are given on art historical topics at least 10 evenings during the year. They are announced in the local newspaper. Reservations are necessary.

The *Bookstore* sells a guidebook for $2, a book on the museum's herb garden and fine art reproductions of paintings in the collections. There is also a good selection of art books and gift items.

Parking is available; however, advance parking reservations are recommended for guaranteed parking and admission on a specific date for morning or after-noon arrival. Write or call the reservations office. No visitors will be admitted if they have parked outside the museum grounds. Visitors arriving by taxi, bicycle or bus will be admitted without a reservation. Bus passengers must request a museum pass from the driver.

Main Level   The *Garden Tea Room* serves a cafeteria-style lunch from 10:30 A.M. to 2:30 P.M. and desserts and beverages until 3:30 P.M.

Hours: *October to May:* Tuesday–Saturday, 10 A.M.–5 P.M. *June to Septem-ber:* Monday–Friday, 10 A.M.–5 P.M. *Closed:* Sundays, Christmas, New Year's, Washington's Birthday, Memorial Day, July 4, Labor Day, Thanksgiving.

Admission: No charge for museum or parking.

MONTEREY

MONTEREY PENINSULA MUSEUM OF ART
559 Pacific St.
Monterey, CA 93940
Tel: (408)372-5477

Founded in 1959, the Spanish-style museum, with its red tile roof, occupies the upper two floors of a three-story building erected in the 1920s. The collection of regional art and international folk art is displayed on a rotating basis in five small galleries, hallways and office areas. Two galleries are of special interest to those exploring the history of artists on the Monterey Peninsula.

Exterior view. Courtesy Monterey Peninsula Museum of Art, Monterey

SAMPLING THE COLLECTION

GEORGE INNESS American, 1825–1894 *Approaching Storm* Oil **Outside of Gift Shop**

Inness's early landscapes were influenced by the Hudson River School. His mature ones rendered in a more tranquil, personal and lyrical style were suffused by silver tones imitative of Corot.

JACOB EPSTEIN American/British, 1880–1959 *Portrait of Terrenia (Mrs. Gerrard)* 1929 Bronze bust **Next to Front Desk**

Rita Romilly 1937 Bronze head

Although Epstein's portrait sculptures seem quite traditional today, they were controversial when they first appeared. Epstein, influenced by Rodin, produced insightful decisive portraits in an Impressionistic style.

DONALD TEAGUE American, b. 1897 *Arab Market* 1977 Watercolor **In Front of Front Desk**

Teague is a regional artist, a watercolorist of realistic landscapes who occasionally paints in oil.

FACILITIES

Changing Exhibitions are regularly featured in the main and balcony galleries.

The *Library* houses art books, catalogs and magazines.

The *Gift Shop's* most popular items are folk art objects and note cards. Also on sale are selections from a jade collection. Prices range from 50¢ to $500.

Hours: Tuesday–Friday, 10 A.M.–4 P.M.; Saturday–Sunday, 1 P.M.–4 P.M. Closed: Mondays, holidays.

Admission: Free.

NEWPORT BEACH

NEWPORT HARBOR ART MUSEUM
850 San Clemente Dr.
Newport Beach, CA 92660
Tel: (714)759-1122

The museum was founded in 1961 in the turn-of-the-century Balboa Pavilion. After some years it moved to larger quarters in Newport Beach's colorful pier area. Its latest home, opened in 1977, houses three exhibition galleries designed to present contemporary art in a simple nondistracting environment. It focuses on art from the present and recent past from both our own and other cultures. The permanent collection, only recently begun, emphasizes modern American art.

SAMPLING THE COLLECTION

The Dorothy Sullivan Gallery and the museum lobby are used to display works on a rotating basis.

JIM DINE   *Palette—Self-Portrait No. 1*
American, b. 1935   1964
                                                  Oil and collage on canvas

Dine, a Pop artist, frequently included tangible objects in his paintings. Clothing, household appliances, etc., were often incorporated with great ingenuity.

RON DAVIS   *#550—Unfold and Arc*
American, b. 1937   1977
                                                  Vinyl, acrylic, copolymer, dry
                                                  pigment on canvas

This contemporary California artist deals with the illusion of space through geometric line and color.

JOSEF ALBERS   *Homage to the Square,*
German/American, 1888–1976   *Dry Season*
                                                  1967
                                                  Oil on board

Albers is best known for his *Homage to the Square* series, squares within squares painted in related color creating illusions of still other color. He especially influenced the Op artists of the 1960s.

DAVID PARK   *Bather with Knee Up*
American, 1911–1960   1957
                                                  Oil on canvas

At first painting in the WPA project, then turning to abstraction, Park eventually returned to figure painting to become the leader of the San Francisco Bay Area Figurative movement.

FACILITIES

Lectures are offered on topical art issues, current exhibitions, art history and subjects of related interest.

Changing Exhibitions of the work of a variety of artists is a regular museum feature.

Films are shown on art-related subjects.

The *Museum Bookshop* offers a selection of art books, postcards, note cards, handcrafted jewelry and bibelots.

The *Art Sales Gallery* displays a continuous and changing exhibition of works of art for sale. Rental is to members only.

The *Sculpture Garden Restaurant* is a pleasant dining facility.

Hours: Tuesday–Sunday, 12 P.M.–4 P.M.; Friday evening, 6 P.M.–9 P.M. *Closed:* Mondays, New Year's, Easter, Memorial Day, July 4, Thanksgiving, Christmas.

Admission: Free. However, there is a donation box.

OAKLAND

MILLS COLLEGE ART GALLERY
Oakland, CA 94613
Tel: (415)632-2700, ext. 310

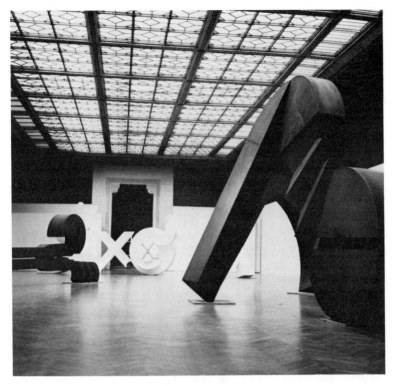

Interior Gallery. *Courtesy Mills College Art Gallery, Oakland*

Built in 1925 to blend with the terrain, the Spanish-style gallery of steel reinforced concrete has a skylit ceiling. It was a very modern structure. The most
extensive holdings in the permanent collection, parts of which are usually on
view, are represented by approximately 3,000 works from the 12th century to
contemporary Masters. The Prieto Gallery, also on campus, shows selections
of ceramics and glass.

SAMPLING THE COLLECTION

Since the following works are rotated for exhibition they may not always be on
view.

AUGUSTE RODIN   *Standing Nude*
French, 1840–1917   Pencil and watercolor
In addition to being an outstanding sculptor, Rodin executed tinted drawings in
which abstracted forms, light and dark tones, and fine draftsmanship are evi-
dent.

LAZLO MOHOLY-NAGY   *CH XI*
Hungarian, 1895–1946   1939
                                           Oil on canvas
Moholy taught at the Bauhaus. His paintings, influenced by his Constructivist
sculptures, were grounded in principles of the Machine Age.

IMOGEN CUNNINGHAM   *Magnolia Blossom*
American, 1884–1976   1925
                           Photograph
Cunningham was one of America's leading portrait photographers and print-
makers. She preferred simple darkroom procedures but often used complex
printing techniques.

President's   EMIL NOLDE   *Tulips and Calla Lily*
House   German, 1876–1956   Watercolor
Nolde was an expressionist whose tormented paintings were executed in stri-
dent colors. In his watercolors he attempted to depict his feelings about nature.

President's   WINSLOW HOMER   *Longing (Waiting for Dad)*
House   American, 1836–1910   Watercolor
Homer was self-taught and little influenced by others. Watercolor was a favorite
medium throughout his career. The simple charm of his early work was expressed in genre scenes in a realistic style.

On Extended   DIEGO RIVERA   *Mother and Child*
Loan   Mexican, 1886–1957   1926
                                             Oil on canvas
While living in Europe, Rivera was influenced by Cubism. Upon returning to
Mexico he adopted a style that leaned heavily on the Mayan and Aztec past.

FACILITIES

One Person shows as well as selections from other collections in the area are
presented.

A *small selection* of prints and cards are for sale in the gallery.

Hours: *Mills College Art Gallery:* Wednesday–Sunday, 12 P.M.–4 P.M. *Prieto
Gallery:* Monday–Friday, 9 A.M.–4 P.M.

Admission: Free.

OAKLAND MUSEUM
1000 Oak St.
Oakland, CA 94607
Tel: (415)273-3402

The Oakland Museum is housed in a beautiful three-tiered complex of terraces,
gardens and galleries designed by the firm of Kevin Roche, John Dinkeloo and
Associates. It occupies four city blocks, 7.7 acres, and is actually three museums
in one. It tells the story of California through its art, history and natural sciences.

SAMPLING THE COLLECTION

The art gallery features extensive collections of paintings, prints, sculpture,
photography and decorative arts either by California artists or artists dealing
with California subjects.

Gallery of   ALBERT BIERSTADT   *The Yosemite Valley*
California   American, 1830–1902   1868
Art,   Oil on canvas
Level III   Bierstadt was tremendously popular for his large-scale paintings of American

scenery. His lighting was theatrical and his surface textures meticulously wrought.

GEORGE INNESS American, 1825–1894	*California* 1894 Oil on canvas	**Gallery of California Art**

Inness was a landscape painter who was mostly self-trained. His mature work is similar to that of the Impressionists.

ARTHUR AND LUCIA MATHEWS American, 20th c.	*Paintings and Furniture* ca. 1890–1920	**Gallery of California Art**

This installation is in the California decorative style.

LARRY BELL American, b. 1939	*Untitled* 1967 Coated glass, Plexiglas and metal stripping	**Gallery of California Art**

Bell is a Minimal sculptor who expresses himself in simple and transparent geometric shapes.

RICHARD DIEBENKORN American, b. 1922	*Figure on Porch* 1959 Oil on canvas	**Gallery of California Art**

Commencing his career as an Abstract Expressionist, Diebenkorn turned to representational work. Later he borrowed from both styles.

MARK DI SUVERO American, b. 1933	*Homage to Charlie Parker* 1978 Steel	**Rishell Court**

Di Suvero's sculptures are composed of found and industrial objects that have a worn quality.

Mark di Suvero, Homage to Charlie Parker. *Courtesy Oakland Museum, Oakland*

Cowell Hall of California History, Level II

ARTIFACTS AND MEMORABILIA FROM FOUR CULTURAL PHASES

The Indian era, prehistoric to Spanish colonization; the Spanish-Mexican period, from early explorations to the mission and rancho cultures; the American period from the arrival of adventurers and explorers to the 1906 earthquake; and the 20th century.

California Kitchen
1850s

This kitchen, from a gold-rush town, contains a wood-burning stove, cast-iron cooking pots, handmade cupboards, a manufactured dropleaf table, children's toys, and is built of sugar-pine planks.

Pioneer Car
1893–1896

Built by a San Francisco machinist for his own use, this was the first motor vehicle manufactured in California. The car, in nearly its original condition, has a wooden frame and a sliding gear system.

Fire Pumper
1890s

The American-La France steam-pumper fire engine was built in Elmira, New York, and used by the Oakland Fire Department from 1898 to 1921. It was drawn by two horses.

DESIGNED BY C. A. BECK AND
HENRY GORHAM

Schmidt Window
1922

The art glass window, created to commemorate the 50th anniversary of Max Schmidt's founding of San Francisco's Schmidt Lithograph Company, graced the tower lobby of the firm until ownership changed in 1966.

Cowell Hall of California History, Level II

PERFUME FACTORY (1930s)

The raw material and finished products, having Hawaiian-inspired names, indicate that the small laboratory-factory of Paul and Estrellita Jones was among the first to capitalize on Hawaii's glamorous image.

Museum, Level I

THE HALL OF CALIFORNIA (ECOLOGY)

The interrelated life activities of plants and animals within each of California's eight biotic zones are arranged to allow visitors to take a simulated walk across California. The exhibit re-creates natural habitats. Biotic zones in the Natural Sciences gallery are Coastline, Coast Mountains, Inner Coast, Interior Valley, Sierran Slope, High Sierra, Great Basin and Desert.

FACILITIES

Public Tours leave gallery information desks on each level weekdays, 2 P.M., on weekends, as announced. Group arrangements may also be made for museum-wide tours, total communication tours for the deaf, afternoon senior citizens' tea and tours, and special Indian theme tours which visit all galleries. For further information, phone (415)273-3515.

Changing Exhibitions of the work of a variety of artists is a regular museum feature.

The *Snack Bar* serves soup, sandwiches, salads, and beverages. It is open Tuesday–Friday, 10 A.M.–3 P.M., Saturday–Sunday, 12 P.M.–4 P.M.

The *Restaurant,* overlooking the gardens and reflecting pond, offers a changing menu and service. It is open Tuesday–Friday, two seatings, 11:45 A.M. and 1 P.M. Reservations suggested. Call (415)834-2329.

The *Collectors Gallery* contains a selection of prints, paintings, ceramics, glass- **Lower Level** ware, jewelry and wood at prices that make these original works by leading **Entrance off** northern California artists tremendously appealing. Sales and rentals. **Main Lobby**

The *Museum Store* offers unusual books and calendars, handmade jewelry, **Lower Level,** prints, museum catalogs, textiles, cards, toys and games. The prices start at **Main Lobby** $1.50.

Films, Lectures and *Performing Arts* are offered in the museum theater. **Lower Level**

Parking is available in the museum garage 8 A.M.–6 P.M. daily or until late programs have been concluded. Rate is 25¢ per hour; 50¢ evenings. Entrances on Oak and 12th Streets.

Hours: Tuesday–Saturday, 10 A.M.–5 P.M.; Sunday, 12 P.M.–7 P.M. *Closed:* Mondays, Thanksgiving, Christmas, New Year's.

Admission: Free (admission is charged for some changing exhibitions).

PALM SPRINGS

PALM SPRINGS DESERT MUSEUM
101 Museum Dr.
Palm Springs, CA 92262
Tel: (714)325-7186

The contemporary architecture of the museum, with its sunken sculpture gardens and splashing fountains, is compatible with the desert surroundings. The building houses an art collection and one of natural science. Although the art collection numbers nearly 700 pieces of sculpture, paintings and tapestries, emphasis is placed on California art with a secondary interest in Western American art. The natural science wing is dedicated to the collection, preservation and demonstration of the natural sciences and anthropology, particularly of the immediate Coachella Valley region. It contains almost 1,300 American Indian artifacts, including examples of rug-making and basketry.

SAMPLING THE COLLECTION

HENRY MOORE   *Reclining Figure*   **Weiner**
British, b. 1898   1956   **Sculpture**
                          Bronze   **Terrace at**
                                                    Museum
                          Torso of Woman   **Entrance**
                          1957
                          Bronze

                          Reclining Figure #3
                          1961
                          Bronze

Moore has always been interested in the reclining figure, which he expresses in energetic style and monumental size. His anthropomorphic forms seem to grow out of the material he uses.

Weiner MARINO MARINI   *The Warrior*
Sculpture Italian, 1901–1980   1959–1960
Terrace   Bronze

After the 1930s, Marini favored the archaic Greek theme of horse and rider. With passing years his figures became increasingly attenuated and the execution more emotional.

FACILITIES

Lectures, Films, Concerts, Dance and *Drama* programs are frequently offered.

Temporary Exhibitions culled from the museum's collection or *Loan Exhibitions* from other institutions are regular features of the museum's changing program.

The *Museum Shop's* most popular items are pottery, jewelry and books with prices ranging from $3 to $100.

Hours: Tuesday–Saturday, 10 A.M.–5 P.M.; Sunday, 1 P.M.–5 P.M. *Closed:* Mondays, legal holidays.

Admission: Adults, $1.50; members, students, children, free.

PASADENA

NORTON SIMON MUSEUM
Colorado and Orange Grove Blvds.
Pasadena, CA 91105
Tel: (213)449-6840

First founded in 1924 as the Pasadena Museum of Modern Art, the museum was reorganized under the leadership of Norton Simon. The contemporary structure built in 1969 was then internally remodeled and reopened in 1975. The art on exhibition contains a majority of works from the collections of the Norton Simon Foundations. The collections include European paintings spanning six centuries; one of the largest Indian and Southeast Asian sculpture collections outside of Asia; monumental 19th- and 20th-century European sculpture and a comprehensive assemblage of graphic works by Goya, Rembrandt and Picasso.

SAMPLING THE COLLECTION

Gallery 2A CONSTANTIN BRANCUSI   *Bird in Space*
Rumanian/French, 1876–1957   1931
                                                    Polished bronze

Brancusi refined natural shapes to such perfection that they represent an ideal image. *Bird in Space* was so controversial that the U.S. Customs Bureau rejected it as an artwork.

Gallery 3 RAPHAEL (RAFFAELO SANZIO)   *Madonna and Child with Book*
Italian, Umbrian, 1483–1520   ca. 1504
                                                     Oil on panel

Exterior view. Courtesy Norton Simon Museum, Pasadena

This painting was executed early in Raphael's career. Already recognized as an equal of Leonardo da Vinci and Michelangelo, he was a leading contributor to High Renaissance art in which harmony and balance were contained in Classical realism.

HANS MEMLING
German/Flemish, ca. 1435–1494

The Blessing Christ
1478
Oil on panel

Gallery 4

Much of Memling's work was influenced by Rogier van der Weyden. His religious paintings had a serene quality with his subjects portrayed quite like the everyday folk in his portraits.

DESIDERIO DA SETTIGNANO
Italian, ca. 1430–1464

Beauregard Madonna
ca. 1455
Marble

Gallery 4

Desiderio's low reliefs were remarkable for their delicate effects and meticulous design.

FLEMISH

*The Madonna and Child Enthroned
with Mary Cleopathas and Mary
Salome and a Chorus of Angels*
ca. 1515
Wool

Gallery 4

The Justice of the Emperor Trajan
ca. 1510
Wool and silk

Tapestries were considered precious furnishings and used for decorative and commemorative purposes. The subjects were mostly religious and historical. These tapestries were woven for Louis XII of France.

Gallery 6   FRANCISCO DE ZURBARAN   *Still Life: Lemons, Oranges*
Spanish, 1598–ca. 1664   *and a Rose*
                                 1633
                                 Oil on canvas

Zurbarán's Baroque paintings of clear but subdued color were set against dark backgrounds. Most of his work was of religious subjects.

Gallery 7   REMBRANDT HARMENSZ VAN RIJN   *Self-Portrait*
Dutch, 1606–1669   1636
                                 Oil on oak panel

From early in his career to the year of his death Rembrandt painted a series of revealing self-portraits. They record not only his visual appearance but his inner emotions.

                                 Titus
                                 ca. 1653–1654
                                 Oil on canvas

Later portraits, such as this of Rembrandt's son, emphasize light and shadow, while evoking real insight into character.

Gallery 7   FRANS HALS   *Portrait of a Man*
Dutch, 1581–1666   1650–1655
                                 Oil on canvas

Hals is best known for his insouciant portraits executed with great vitality. He captured the moment with broad, vigorous brush strokes and a restricted palette that would influence the Impressionists to follow.

Gallery 8   PETER PAUL RUBENS   *Holy Woman at the Sepulchre*
Flemish, 1577–1640   ca. 1611–1614
                                 Oil on panel

Rubens's composition and figure drawing are influenced by the Italian Renaissance. The intensity of feeling in his paintings is typically Baroque. Devoted to Catholicism, most of his commissions after 1610 were for religious paintings.

Gallery 9   EDOUARD MANET   *The Ragpicker*
French, 1832–1883   ca. 1869
                                 Oil on canvas

Manet's work was frequently rejected by the Salon whose judges were shocked by his subject matter and its execution. A major founder of Impressionism, he never fully accepted its tenets and exhibited independently.

Gallery 9   JACQUES LIPCHITZ   *Bather III*
Lithuanian/American, 1891–1973   1917
                                 Bronze (edition of 7, cast #6)

Gardens   *The Figure*
                                 1926–1930
                                 Bronze

Lipchitz's work evolved from the stolid, blocklike shapes of Cubism to "sculptures transparentes," a more openwork sculpture.

Gallery 10   GEORGES BRAQUE   *Still Life with Pipe*
French, 1882–1963   1912
                                 Oil on canvas

Braque was influenced by the Fauvists and also by Cézanne. He and Picasso were the originators of Cubism.

JUAN GRIS   *Still Life with a Poem*   **Gallery 10**
Spanish, 1887–1927   1915
                                 Oil and collage on canvas
Gris incorporated bits of flat materials in his Cubist paintings. These collage additions give his work a tangible reality.

VINCENT VAN GOGH   *Mulberry Tree*   **Gallery 10**
Dutch, 1853–1890   1889
                                 Oil on canvas
Van Gogh was a Post-Impressionist painter. His later style incorporated the bold lines of Japanese prints with brilliant, thick color and swirling frantic brushwork.

GIOVANNI BATTISTA TIEPOLO   *The Triumph of Virtue and*   **Gallery 15**
Italian, 1696–1770   *Fortitude*
                                 ca. 1740–1750
                                 Oil on canvas (ceiling)
Tiepolo was the principal Italian Rococo decorative painter of his time adorning villas and churches. His fresco paintings, rendered in a lighter palette and a looser style than earlier, used architectural perspective.

WILHELM LEHMBRUCK   *Standing Woman*   **Gallery 17**
German, 1881–1919   1910
                                 Bronze
Lehmbruck's lean, elongated sculptures convey an inner thoughtfulness while communicating a sense of movement.

PABLO PICASSO   *La Pointe de la Cité*   **Gallery 19**
Spanish, 1881–1973   1912
                                 Oil on canvas

                                 Head of a Woman
                                 1909
                                 Bronze (edition of 9, cast #3)
Picasso's prolific career encompassed many styles and many mediums. This painting and this sculpture from his period of Analytical Cubism allude to the form of an object without actually imitating it.

FRANCISCO GOYA Y LUCIENTES   *La Tauromaquia, Los Caprichios,* **Gallery 26**
Spanish, 1746–1828   *Los Proverbios, Disasters of War*
                                 Etchings
Goya greatly influenced the Impressionists and Expressionists. These 35 etchings, representative of his graphics, express his passionate feeling for the human condition, always grounded in reality but often illustrated in fantasy, satire and caricature.

GEORGES ROUAULT   *Two Nudes (The Sirens)*   **Gallery 29**
French, 1871–1958   1906–1908
                                 Gouache on paper
Although these gouaches were among a series of profane subjects, Rouault painted mostly dark-colored religious themes in Expressionist style influenced by Fauvism and his early training as a stained-glass worker.

AUGUSTE RODIN   *The Burghers of Calais*   **Gardens**
French, 1840–1917   1884–1885
                                 Bronze (edition of 12, cast #10)

Rodin's achievements in sculpture can be likened to those of the Impressionists in art. Parts of figures may be partially finished while others are finely modeled, lending great naturalism to his work.

Gardens   ARISTIDE MAILLOL   *The River*
              French, 1861–1944   1939–1943
                                                   Lead (artist's proof)
Maillol based his sculptures of mature, nude women on the ideals of ancient Greek art. His immobile figures of monumental proportions changed little over the course of his career.

Gardens   HENRY MOORE   *King and Queen*
              British, b. 1898   1952–1953
                                                   Bronze (edition of 4, cast #1)
Since 1945 Moore has worked mostly in bronze. This work, with its lean figures and geometric heads, has Surrealist overtones founded in early Mediterranean sculpture.

Galleries   *THE GALKA SCHEYER COLLECTION OF THE BLUE FOUR*
28, 30
The "Blue Four" (Jawlensky, Feininger, Kandinsky, Klee) were a splinter group of the "Blue Rider," a Munich based group. They reorganized after World War I to exhibit their paintings of diverse Abstract Expressionist styles abroad. This collection offers a variety of media, including oil, gouache, watercolor, ink, pencil.

FACILITIES

The *Bookshop* stocks—in addition to books—posters, prints and cards. All paid visitors are given a free reproduction of one of the masterpieces in the museum.

Parking is ample and free.

Hours: Thursday–Sunday, 12 P.M.–6 P.M. *Open most holidays except Thanksgiving, Christmas, New Year's. Closed:* Monday–Wednesday.

Admission: Adults, $2; students, senior citizens, 75¢; children under 12 free, when accompanied by an adult.

SACRAMENTO

CROCKER ART MUSEUM
(FORMERLY E. B. CROCKER ART GALLERY)
216 O St.
Sacramento, CA 95814
Tel: (916)446-4677

The museum, opened in 1875 by Edwin Bryant Crocker adjacent to his home, houses his collection of approximately 700 paintings. The building, designed in the style of a 16th-century villa, contains a ballroom and formerly housed a billiard room, two bowling alleys and a roller-skating rink. Except for the decorative interior painting (which is in the process of being restored) all the interior decoration is original. The actual Crocker home was later remodeled into a museum annex and, more recently, the R. A. Herold Wing was added to furnish changing exhibition space and a gallery for the museum's growing contemporary art collection. The museum's collections range from ancient to modern times and come from all over the world. In addition to the original Crocker collection there is Greek, Roman and pre-Columbian art; Korean ceramics; Chinese art from the 7th through the 19th centuries; Japanese art; works of California artists and over 1,200 drawings and watercolors by major Masters.

SAMPLING THE COLLECTION

BERNARDO STROZZI Italian, 1581–1644	*Prophet Elijah and the* *Widow* ca. 1635 Oil on canvas	**European** **Gallery**

Strozzi was a Capuchin friar whose early work was strongly influenced by Rubens. Once settled in Venice, he adopted a lighter palette in the execution of religious and genre painting.

GASPER DE CRAEYER Flemish, 1582–1669	*The Nativity* Oil on canvas	**European** **Gallery**

De Craeyer was respected by his contemporaries and sought after by the courts of Brussels and Spain. He was devoted to his own standards of style.

CHARLES C. NAHL American	*Sunday Morning in the* *Mines* Oil on canvas	**Upstairs** **Foyer of** **Crocker Art**

Nahl was a genre painter whose depictions of California life formed the interpre- **Gallery** tation of historic subjects for many in future generations.

Wayne Thiebaud, Boston Cremes. *Courtesy Crocker Art Museum, Sacramento*

American   THOMAS HILL   *Great Canyon of the Sierras—*
Gallery   American, 1829–1908   *Yosemite*
                                                Oil on canvas
Hill, a California landscapist, was first influenced by the Hudson River School. After studying in Paris his work became less grandiose, employing the softer forms of the French Barbizon School.

Herold Wing,   WAYNE THIEBAUD   *Boston Cremes*
Contemporary   American, b. 1920   Oil on canvas
Gallery   Thiebaud, a Pop artist, paints still lifes of cafeteria-produced baking goods with heavy impasto of rich color.

FACILITIES

Guided Tours are offered to school and adult groups by reservation.

Lectures are frequently scheduled.

Changing Exhibitions of the work of a variety of artists is a regular museum feature.

The *Museum Shop* has the largest selection of art books in the region. Also on sale are stained glass and jewelry, greeting cards, cookbooks, gift wares, post-cards of the collection and catalogs of exhibitions organized by the museum.

Ballroom   *Concerts* and *Recitals* are held on Sunday afternoons.

Hours: Wednesday–Sunday, 10 A.M.–5 P.M.; Tuesday, 2 P.M.–10 P.M. *Closed:* Mondays, Thanksgiving, Christmas, New Year's.

Admission: Adults, 50¢; children under 12, free.

SAN DIEGO

SAN DIEGO MUSEUM OF ART
Balboa Park
San Diego, CA 92101
Tel: (714)232-7931

Built in Spanish plateresque style, the San Diego Museum of Art is located in Balboa Park. Its collections include Italian Renaissance and Spanish Baroque paintings, Oriental art from 1000 B.C. to A.D. 1900, American art from 1750 to 1900 and contemporary art and sculpture.

SAMPLING THE COLLECTION

Baroque   JUAN SANCHEZ-COTAN   *Quince, Cabbage, Melon and*
Gallery 16   Spanish, 1561–1627   *Cucumbers*
                                               ca. 1602–1603
                                               Oil on canvas
Spanish Baroque painting was influenced by both Italian and Flemish art. A synthesis of scrupulous realism and abstract form lend harmony and simplicity to this painting by one of the first Spanish Masters of still life.

ANTHONY VAN DYCK
Flemish, 1599–1641

Queen Henrietta Maria
ca. 1638–1639
Oil on canvas

Dutch and
English
Gallery 17

At the outset of his career Van Dyck was chief assistant to Rubens, who greatly influenced his style. He is best known for his flattering portraits of the aristocracy.

HENRY MOORE
English, b. 1898

Reclining Figure: Arch Leg
1969
Bronze

Sculpture
Garden

Inspired by primitive cultures and organic phenomena, Moore's work has great vigor. The forms he creates are determined by the materials he uses.

Exterior view. Courtesy San Diego Museum of Art, San Diego

FACILITIES

Guided Tours, Lectures, Films, Concerts are offered. Inquire about schedule.

Changing Exhibitions of the work of a variety of artists is a regular museum feature.

A *Restaurant* is located nearby in Balboa Park.

The *Sales Shop* sells books, postcards, reproductions of paintings suitable for framing, as well as original works of handcrafted jewelry and pottery.

The *Art Sales and Rental Gallery* offers original works by local, national and international artists.

Hours: Tuesday–Sunday, 10 A.M.–5 P.M.. *Closed:* Mondays, New Year's, July 4, Thanksgiving, Christmas.

Admission: Adults, $1; children with adults, free; children without adults, 50¢; members, free. Tuesday, free.

TIMKEN ART GALLERY
Balboa Park
San Diego, CA 92101
Tel: (714)239-5548

Two sisters, Anne and Amy Putnam, created the Putnam Foundation in 1951 in order to perpetuate the purchase of art in their own names. The Timken Art Gallery was built to house their collection and opened its doors in 1965. It is a classically simple one-story building of bronze and travertine and shares the plaza of Balboa Park with the San Diego Museum of Art. Six galleries are at either side of a central rotunda lit by natural daylight. Often referred to as a jewel box because of its small size and the quality of its collection, it contains European and American art from the 13th to the 20th centuries.

Exterior view. Courtesy Timken Art Gallery, San Diego

SAMPLING THE COLLECTION

The gallery is small and all on one floor. The guards will be happy to point out the following works.

REMBRANDT HARMENSZ VAN RIJN   *Saint Bartholomew*
Dutch, 1606–1669   1657
                                Oil on canvas
Rembrandt often painted holy men whom he endowed with a mystery removed from daily Dutch life. Light in opposition to the large dark areas and the thickly pigmented brushwork express a great poignancy.

PIETER BRUEGHEL, THE ELDER   *Parable of the Sower*
Flemish, ca. 1525–1569   1557
                             Oil on panel
Brueghel's insight into human nature, his attention to detail and his ability to capture a moment in time were hallmarks of his work. This is the first of many parables he painted.

PETRUS CHRISTUS   *The Dormition of the Virgin*
Flemish, ca. 1410–ca. 1472   ca. 1455–1460
                             Oil on panel
Christus's northern conception of this theme has a solid and placid quality.

PHILIPPE DE CHAMPAIGNE   *Christ Healing the Blind*
Flemish, 1602–1674   Oil on canvas
Champaigne was a deeply religious man whose strong attachment to the Jansenist movement is reflected in this Counter-Reformation allegory of Christ purifying the Church.

JEAN-HONORE FRAGONARD   *Blind Man's Bluff*
French, 1732–1806   Oil on canvas
Fragonard's paintings, executed with great charm and gaiety, conveyed the carefree activities of the nobility before the French Revolution.

PAOLO CALIARI VERONESE   *Madonna and Child with*
Italian, Venetian, 1528–1588 *St. Elizabeth, The Infant*
                              St. John, and St. Justina
                              ca. 1555–1560
                              Oil on canvas
St. Justina was much worshiped in Padua and Venice. It is highly possible that this painting was executed for her church in Venice. Veronese's work epitomized the Venetian style.

GABRIEL METSU   *The Love Letter*
Dutch, 1629–1667   1655–1660
                   Oil on panel
Metsu painted portraits, history and genre works valuing accurate representation.

THE MAGDALENE MASTER,   *Dossal with Virgin and Child*
1265–1290   *and Angels, and Twelve Scenes*
AND UNNAMED FLORENTINE   *of the Passion*
MASTER
Italian
The Magdalene Master painted the central figures, the Unnamed Florentine Master, the smaller ones. We see the beginning of a naturalist style soon to become popular in 14th-century Florence.

EASTMAN JOHNSON   *The Cranberry Harvest, Island*
American, 1824–1906   *of Nantucket*
                      1880

Influenced by earlier Dutch genre scenes, Johnson's paintings are forthright evocations of ordinary events.

RUSSIAN   *The Royal Doors*
                                                 Icon
In Russian churches the Royal Door with its religious paintings was the central one of three that allowed entry into the altar area.

FACILITIES

Guided Tours are available on Wednesday and Thursday.

Hours: Tuesday–Saturday, 10 A.M.–4:30 P.M.; Sunday, 1:30 P.M.–4:30 P.M.
         Closed: Mondays, national holidays, September.

Admission: Free.

SAN FRANCISCO

ASIAN ART MUSEUM OF SAN FRANCISCO
AVERY BRUNDAGE COLLECTION
Golden Gate Park
San Francisco, CA 94118
Tel: (415)558-2993

The museum houses over 10,000 sculptures, architectural elements, paintings, bronzes, ceramics, jades and decorative objects illustrating all the major periods and stylistic developments of the arts of Asia, from Turkey to Japan, and from Mongolia to Indonesia. Avery Brundage amassed 95 percent of it. The collection is noted for the quality of its individual pieces.

SAMPLING THE COLLECTION

1st Floor   *MAGNIN JADE ROOM*

Includes a unique display of Chinese jades and hardstones dating from the Neolithic period to the 20th century.

1st Floor   *CHINESE BRONZE GALLERIES*

One of the foremost collections of Chinese bronzes in the world, illustrating every major type, phase and style in the art of Bronze Age China from the Shang Dynasty (ca. 1523–1028 B.C.) to the Han (206 B.C.–A.D. 220).

1st Floor   *CHINESE CERAMICS*

A particularly comprehensive collection covering all representative types from the Neolithic period to the 20th century. It is augmented by pieces from the Roy Leventritt collection of blue and white porcelains.

1st Floor   *CHINESE LACQUERS*

The collection contains pieces dating from the Chou Dynasty (ca. 1027–256 B.C.) to the Ch'ing (1644–1912), with important Sung (907–1279), Yüan (1279–1368) and Ming (1368–1644) examples.

"Tsun" Ritual Vessel in the Shape of a Rhinoceros. *Courtesy Asian Art Museum of San Francisco, The Avery Brundage Collection*

CHINESE SCULPTURE
1st Floor

The collection contains a large number of important dated and undated sculptures and features the earliest dated Chinese Buddhist statue in the world (A.D. 338.)

CHINESE PAINTINGS
1st Floor

Hand scrolls, hanging scrolls, album leaves and fans date from the Sung Dynasty to modern times.

INDIAN, AFGHANISTAN, AND NEPALESE-TIBETAN-INDIAN ART
2nd Floor

These galleries highlight regional styles in stone sculpture and bronzes dating from the 3rd to the 15th centuries. The Hoysala Ganesh (carved stone god) is the finest outside of India.

TIBETAN GALLERIES
2nd Floor

Here are housed statues, ritual paraphernalia and Tibetan tankas.

SOUTHEAST ASIAN ART
2nd Floor

These galleries contain outstanding Khmer sculpture, plus important sculpture from Champa, Java and other areas, along with Thai ceramics dating from prehistoric times to the 15th century.

KOREAN AND JAPANESE ART
2nd Floor

Statuary, ceramics, painting, lacquer and decorative arts are all represented here.

IRANIAN ART
Around Balcony

On view are Luristan bronzes, prehistoric pottery, vessels from Giyan, Sialk and "Amlash" areas, Islamic ceramics and metalwork.

FACILITIES

Daily Tours by trained guides are available.

Lectures are offered from time to time. For information call (415)387-5922.

Special Loan Exhibitions from other museums or private collections are shown once or twice a year.

The *Library* contains, in addition to books and periodicals, photographs, microfilms and slides. It is open 1 P.M.–4:45 P.M. weekdays except holidays.

The *Japan Center Extension* is located on the Webster Street Bridge in Japan Center, San Francisco. Open 10 A.M.–10 P.M. seven days a week. Objects are rotated three times a year, and information about the art is provided in bilingual (Japanese/English) labels.

The *Café de Young* and the *Japanese Tea Garden* are open daily 10 A.M.– 4 P.M..

Adjoining the Museum   The *Museum Society Bookshop* offers publications, postcards and slides illustrating various segments of the museum's collections. The popular handbooks of the collections range in price from $5 to $10.

Hours: Open daily, 10 A.M.–5 P.M. except Christmas and New Year's.

Admission: First day of each month is free. Adults (18–64), 75¢; youths (12–17), 25¢; senior (65 and over), free; children (under 12), free; members and recognized educational groups are free.

FINE ARTS MUSEUMS OF SAN FRANCISCO

M. H. DE YOUNG MEMORIAL MUSEUM
Golden Gate Park
8th Ave. at Kennedy Dr.
San Francisco, CA 94121
Tel: (415)558-2887

CALIFORNIA PALACE OF THE LEGION OF HONOR
Lincoln Park
34th Ave. and Clement St.
San Francisco, CA 94121
Tel: (415)558-2881

Two buildings from the 1894 California Midwinter International Expositions were preserved and expanded to become the M. H. de Young Memorial Museum. The collection's strength lies in its Old Masters paintings; traditional arts of Africa, Oceania and the Americas and American art. Gifted to San Francisco in 1924 by Mr. and Mrs. Adolph Spreckels, the California Palace of the Legion of Honor is a Neoclassical style structure copied from the original Parisian building of the same name. The collection's greatest interest lies in its 18th-century French paintings; the Louis XVI room interior from the Hotel d'Humières in Paris and the Rodin sculptures from 1889 to 1917 that grace the central court. In 1970, the museums were merged under the leadership of a single director but each maintains its own flavor.

Pierre Auguste Renoir, Mother and Child. *By permission of the Fine Arts Museums of San Francisco*

SAMPLING THE COLLECTION

RAFAELLINO DEL GARBO
Italian, Florentine, ca. 1466–ca. 1525

Enthroned Madonna with Saints Jerome and Bartholomew
1502
Oil on panel

Rafaellino, a painter of the High Renaissance, was influenced by Filippino Lippi, most likely his teacher. A variety of styles suggests that more than one artist might be responsible for his work.

EL GRECO (DOMENICOS THEOTOCOPOULOS)
Greek, 1541–1614

Saint John the Baptist
1597–1602
Oil on canvas

The nervous tension in El Greco's later works, along with his eerie color contrasts and attenuated figures, created a style so mystical and personal that he had no immediate followers.

Georges de La Tour, Portrait of an Old Woman. *By permission of the Fine Arts Museums of San Francisco*

PETER PAUL RUBENS
Flemish, 1577–1640

Portrait of Rogier Clarisse
1611
Oil on canvas

The Tribute Money
ca. 1612
Oil on wood panel

During this period, Rubens, the foremost painter of the northern Baroque, evolved his own personal style, less intensely dramatic than before, enabling numerous assistants to work on his varied *oeuvre*.

REMBRANDT HARMENSZ VAN RIJN
Dutch, 1606–1669

Joris de Caullery
Canvas

Rembrandt used light and shadow while carefully detailing his subjects' facial composition and expression to create psychologically insightful portraits.

GEORGES DE LA TOUR
French, 1593–1652

Portrait of an Old Man
Oil on canvas

Portrait of an Old Woman
Oil on canvas

La Tour rendered simple, sharply defined figures in religious and genre scenes of noble quality, harmoniously constructed.

JOSHUA REYNOLDS
British, 1723–1792

The Marchioness of Townsend
Oil on canvas

Reynolds, one of the most important British portraitists, was extremely popular in his own day, equally comfortable with aristocrats and literary and theatrical figures. His portraits often incorporated Classical and learned references.

NICOLAS DE LARGILLIERE
French, 1656–1746

Portrait of a Nobleman
1710
Oil on canvas

Although this portrait is of a nobleman, de Largillière painted mainly the upper middle class, individually and in groups. Set against atmospheric landscapes they presaged the Rococo style to follow.

FRANCOIS BOUCHER
French, 1703–1770

Vertumnus and Pomona
Oil on canvas

Boucher's work typified French 18th-century taste. This scene reflects the frivolity of aristocratic life rather than that of its mythological inspiration. Pinks and blues were favored in his Rococo representations.

JEAN-BAPTISTE CAMILLE COROT
French, 1796–1875

View of Rome
Oil on canvas

Corot traveled in Italy developing a style dependent upon tonal values for its sensitive handling. These atmospheric, lyrical compositions, carefully organized and suffused with a silvery-green haze, were widely copied.

FREDERIC EDWIN CHURCH
American, 1826–1900

Rainy Season in the Tropics
Oil on canvas

Church, a member of the Hudson River School of landscapists, enjoyed great success in his lifetime. He traveled widely, capturing light and atmosphere on canvas in careful treatments of natural panoramas.

PIERRE AUGUSTE RENOIR
French, 1841–1919

Mother and Child
Oil on canvas

Renoir was one of the originators of Impressionism. His broken brush strokes were applied from a colorful palette that excluded black and favored pinks and reds, minimizing his attention to outline.

PAUL CEZANNE
French, 1839–1906

*The Rocks in the Park of the
Château Noir*
ca. 1900
Oil on canvas

In his own words, Cézanne attempted "to make of Impressionism something solid and durable. . . ." In modeling with color to express the geometric forms beneath surfaces, he laid the groundwork for Cubism.

FACILITIES

M. H. de Young Memorial Museum

Tours of the American collections are offered daily at 2:30 P.M.; of the ancient and European collections, 1:30 P.M.; Africa, Oceania and the Americas, 2:00 P.M.

Lectures are presented frequently by eminent authorities in the arts or related fields.

Temporary Exhibitions culled from the museum's collection or *Loan Exhibitions* from other institutions are regular features of the museum's program.

Concerts are held in the galleries or in the Music Concourse.

Children's Programs such as storytelling or lectures with audience participation are often presented.

The *Fine Arts Museum Library* is open to researchers by appointment.

Café de Young, a restaurant with a garden, is open 10 A.M.–4 P.M.

The *Sale Store* features quality merchandise including museum-related items from previous exhibitions along with catalogs, books and posters from these shows.

Art for Touching is offered to the blind or partially sighted as well as to the general public in the gallery of the traditional arts of Africa, Oceania and the Americas. By appointment, (415)387-5122.

Hours: Wednesday–Sunday, 10 A.M.–5 P.M.. *Closed:* Mondays, Tuesdays, New Year's, Christmas.

Admission: Adults (18–64), $1.50; youths (5–17), 50¢; senior citizens (65 and over), 50¢; children under 5, free.

Downtown Art Center

Located at 3 Embarcadero Center, the center offers the business community changing exhibitions, Monday–Friday, 12 P.M.–5 P.M.; Saturday, 12 P.M.–4 P.M.

California Palace of the Legion of Honor

Tours of the permanent collections are available 2 P.M.

Lectures and *Symposia* relating to the exhibitions are presented by eminent art authorities.

A variety of classical music *Concerts* are regularly featured with pipe organ concerts held Saturdays and Sundays, 4 P.M., at no additional charge.

Temporary Exhibitions culled from the museum's collection or *Loan Exhibitions* from other institutions are regular features of the museum's program.

The *Café Chanticleer* serves sandwiches and snacks 10 A.M.–5 P.M.

The *Bookshop* carries postcards and books. Call (415)387-0400.

Hours: Wednesday–Sunday, 10 A.M.–5 P.M. *Closed:* Mondays, Tuesdays, New Year's, Christmas.

Admission: Adults (18–64), $1.50; youths (5–17), 50¢; senior citizens (65 and over), 50¢; children under 5, free.

SAN FRANCISCO MUSEUM OF MODERN ART
Civic Center
Van Ness Ave. at McAllister St.
San Francisco, CA 94102
Tel: (415)863-8800

Dedicated exclusively to modern art, the museum's permanent collection is of importance in appreciating and understanding the work that is being done today. The major periods and influences of 20th-century painting, sculpture, graphics, ceramics and photography are represented in the collection.

SAMPLING THE COLLECTION

HENRI MATISSE   *The Girl with Green Eyes*
French, 1869–1954   1908
                             Oil on canvas
Although this was painted during Matisse's Fauve period, marked by wide brush strokes and vivid color, he sometimes experimented with simpler forms, confining his colors and using a calmer approach.

RICHARD DIEBENKORN   *Cityscape I*
American, b. 1922   1963
                             Oil on canvas
Diebenkorn incorporated some of the Abstract Expressionist techniques of his earlier work when he returned to representational painting.

DIEGO RIVERA   *The Flower Vendor*
Mexican, 1886–1957   1935
                             Oil and tempera on panel
Best known for his murals in which he advanced his nationalistic, social and political beliefs, Rivera executed his easel paintings in the same exuberant and narrative style.

CLYFFORD STILL   *30 Paintings*
American, 1904–1980   1934–1974
Still presented these paintings to the museum in 1975. They represent a complete survey of his work that is unique in a single institution.

FACILITIES

Lectures and Forums featuring prominent persons discussing art-related subjects are often sponsored.

Exhibitions Originated by the Museum or *Loan Exhibitions* from other institutions are the primary features of the museum's program.

Performing Arts programs are offered in poetry reading, dance, jazz, avantgarde and chamber music.

The *Library* has an extensive and international collection of art books, periodicals and exhibition catalogs. Call for hours.

The *Bookshop* carries art books, magazines, games, gift items and a special room for posters and prints. Prices range from $2 to $100.

The *Café* is open Tuesday–Saturday, 10 A.M.–4 P.M.

Parking is available in the garage under the Civic Center Plaza.

Hours: Tuesday, Wednesday, Friday, 10 A.M.–6 P.M.; Thursday, 10 A.M.–10 P.M.; Saturday, Sunday, 10 A.M.–5 P.M. *Closed:* Mondays.

Admission: Adults, $1.25; senior citizens, and those under 16, 75¢.

Exterior view. Courtesy Rosicrucian Egyptian Museum, San Jose

SAN JOSE

ROSICRUCIAN EGYPTIAN MUSEUM
Rosicrucian Park
San Jose, CA 95114
Tel: (408)287-9171

Owned and maintained by the Rosicrucian Order, a worldwide philosophical and cultural organization, the museum is situated in a setting reminiscent of the land of the Nile. It contains the largest collection of Egyptian and Babylonian antiquities in the Western United States and is designed to look like an ancient temple.

SAMPLING THE COLLECTION

Gallery A   BABYLONIAN AND ASSYRIAN   *Cuneiform Tablets*
3000–2000 B.C.
The museum has a fine collection of this early form of writing.

Gallery A   EGYPTIAN   *Statues of Gods*
2000 B.C. to Ptolemaic Period
Bronze
The Egyptian religion of this period was polytheistic. Many of the gods were agents of nature who were feared and worshiped.

| EGYPTIAN | *33 Mummies* | **Gallery B** |

EGYPTIAN *33 Mummies* **Gallery B**
ca. 1090–525 B.C.
The mummies in the collection include cats, birds and gazelles, along with humans.

EGYPTIAN *Replica of an Ancient* **Lower**
Egyptian Rock Tomb **Level off**
ca. 2000 B.C. **Gallery B**
This tomb captures the atmosphere of those of ancient Egypt. It is a composite of many tombs that were carved out of the limestone cliffs. It consists of two chambers, an entry chamber and the burial chamber.

This gallery displays alabaster blocks, offering tables and canopic jars that **Upper Level,** contained the viscera of the mummified person. **Gallery C**

EGYPTIAN JEWELRY COLLECTION **Top Level,**
This collection includes necklaces, bracelets, earrings and scarabs, which were **Gallery D** often used as amulets to ward off evil.

FACILITIES

The *Art Gallery* displays the work of local and international artists.

A *Sales Shop* featuring Egyptian-style jewelry includes ankh rings from as little as 75¢, to $85 for a necklace of silver and semiprecious stones. Coloring books are under $3, and books on Egypt average about $8 each.

A *Planetarium,* Theater of the Sky, examines the mythological traditions and **Science** cosmic roles of the planets and stars. Hours: *June–August:* Daily, 12 P.M.– **Museum** 5 P.M. *September–May:* Saturday–Sunday only, 12 P.M.–5 P.M. Admission: **Building** Adults, $1.50; children, 75¢.

Hours: Tuesday–Friday, 9 A.M.–4:45 P.M.; Saturday–Monday, 12 P.M.–4:45 P.M. *Closed:* New Year's, July 4, August 2, Thanksgiving, Christmas.
Admission: Free.

SAN MARINO

HUNTINGTON LIBRARY, ART GALLERY AND BOTANICAL GARDENS
1151 Oxford Rd.
San Marino, CA 91108
Tel: (213)681-6601

Founded in 1919, in a parklike setting, the Huntington consists of three main parts.

LIBRARY
Houses more than half a million books and five million manuscripts. Nearly 200 special treasures are always on view in the Main Exhibition Hall. They include the Gutenberg Bible (1450–1455), the first book printed in Europe from movable type; the Ellesmere manuscript of Chaucer's *Canterbury Tales* (ca. 1410); some 60 unique literary and historical manuscripts (such as Franklin's *Autobiography* and Thoreau's *Walden*) from the year 1066 to the present; some unique or rare printed books (such as the first printings of Shakespeare's plays), from

View of the Library. *Courtesy Huntington Library, Art Gallery and Botanical Gardens, San Marino*

the 15th century to the present. One wing houses part of the art collection; Renaissance paintings and 18th-century French sculpture, furniture, tapestries and porcelain.

ART GALLERY
Once the Huntington residence, the collection is displayed in domestic settings, similar to those for which the art was created. It is devoted primarily to British and French art of the 18th and 19th centuries, including paintings, drawings, sculpture, silver, miniature portraits, ceramics and furniture.

BOTANICAL GARDENS
Comprised of seven gardens, each of which has an extensive collection of plants. There are shrubs and trees from all over the world, and some plants are in bloom in every season of the year.

SAMPLING THE COLLECTION

ART GALLERY

Main Hall   JEAN-ANTOINE HOUDON   *Diana*
                   French, 1741–1828   1782
                                                Bronze
The *Diana* is one of Houdon's most celebrated works. He is considered the outstanding sculptor of the 18th century.

                                                Portrait of a Lady
                                                1777
                                                Marble
Houdon first gained fame in Rome and then returned to Paris. He became a member of the Academy the same year he executed this work.

THOMAS GAINSBOROUGH	*Blue Boy*	**Main**
British, 1727–1788	ca. 1770	**Gallery**
	Oil on canvas	

Gainsborough first painted landscapes in the 17th-century Dutch tradition. He executed portraits for a living but preferred to paint landscapes. *Blue Boy,* his most famous work, was painted in Bath, a fashionable resort.

| JOSHUA REYNOLDS | *Mrs. Siddons as the* | **Main** |
| British, 1723–1792 | *Tragic Muse* | **Gallery** |

Reynolds, a highly educated man, and major British portraitist, was the first president of the Royal Academy. Although other artists were equally accomplished, none did more to elevate British art.

THOMAS LAWRENCE	*Pinkie*	**Main**
British, 1769–1830	1794	**Gallery**
	Oil on canvas	

Although Lawrence had little formal training, his accomplished style and personal charm made him the most popular portraitist in England. He painted European royalty and heroic figures of the Napoleonic era.

MARTIN CARLIN	*Secretary and Chest*	**Large**
French, act. 1766–1785	ca. 1785	**Drawing**
	Wood	**Room**

Carlin made refined, graceful and elegant furniture for such customers as Marie Antoinette and Madame du Barry. He specialized in lacquered pieces and in tables decorated with Sèvres plaques.

FRENCH	*Savonnerie Carpets*	**Large**
	ca. 1680	**Library**
	Wool	**Room**

During the 17th century, the royal court acquired the Savonnerie factory. Until 1770 only royalty and a few favorites were permitted to purchase the carpets, which had great status value. This carpet was woven for the Grande Galerie of the Louvre.

GIOVANNI DA BOLOGNA	*Nessus and Deianira*	**Small**
Flemish, ca. 1529–1608	ca. 1580	**Library**
	Bronze	**Room**

These statuettes are typical of Giovanni da Bologna's animated sculptures. On Michelangelo's death, with the patronage of the Medici, he became the leading sculptor of Italy.

| ENGLISH | *Drawings and Watercolors* | |
| | early 17th c.– early 20th c. | |

Approximately 12,000 items cover all phases of British draftsmanship.

CONTINENTAL PRINTS

A small collection of about 500 items is particularly rich in fine impressions of the works of Rembrandt and Dürer.

FACILITIES:

Four Tours offered are the *Botanical Gardens* (guided tours of 1 1/2 hours are normally available Tuesday–Friday, 1 P.M.; *Art Gallery* (a taped 45-minute tour is available for renting); *Library* (guided tours of one hour are available Tuesday at 1:15 and for groups by advance arrangement); *Self-Guided Tour Leaflets* (are available for the Art Gallery, the Library, the Central Gardens, the Japanese Garden and the Desert Garden and cost 10 cents each).

The *Bookstore* sells reproductions of many rare and beautiful items from the Huntington collections; illustrations of the gardens and buildings; Christmas and note cards; prints, postcards; 35-mm slides; maps; broadsides; posters; facsimiles; pamphlets; guide booklets and books on English and American history and literature and the arts.

Hours: Tuesday–Saturday, 1 P.M.–4:30 P.M.; Sunday, 12 P.M.–4:30 P.M. Sunday visitors must have advance reservations. Free Sunday tickets may be ordered by sending a stamped, self-addressed envelope to: Sunday Tickets, The Huntington Library, 1151 Oxford Road, San Marino CA 91108. The order must include the number of persons in the group. Applications should reach the Huntington at least seven days in advance of the Sunday requested. Information about ordering Sunday tickets is tape recorded at (213)449-3901. *Closed:* Mondays, major holidays, October.

Admission: Free.

SANTA BARBARA

SANTA BARBARA MUSEUM OF ART
1130 State St.
Santa Barbara, CA 93101
Tel: (805)963-4364

Santa Barbara's Renaissance-style post office was renovated in 1941 and opened as a museum. The landscaped terrace and sidewalk benches provide a tranquil note for the visitor, and a two-story addition has added gallery space. Ludington Court, an inviting area, is entered directly from the street and displays Greek and Roman antiquities from the 6th century B.C. to the 2nd century A.D. Additionally, the collection includes Egyptian antiquities; American paintings from Colonial times to the present; Oriental art; Oriental musical instruments; a doll collection; European and American drawings from the Renaissance to the present and European paintings and sculpture.

SAMPLING THE COLLECTION

Ludington Court GREEK *Lutrophorus* late 4th c. B.C. Marble
This replica of a jar for nuptial water was probably used as a grave marker.

Gould Gallery CLAUDE MONET French, 1840–1926 *Bordighera* 1884 Oil on canvas
Monet was beginning to achieve recognition during this period. *Bordighera* was painted on the Italian coast in the Impressionist style, of which he was the chief and constant proponent.

Morton Gallery AMERICAN *The Buffalo Hunter* Oil
The Buffalo Hunter is one of the country's outstanding examples of American painting.

GEORGIA O'KEEFFE   *Dead Cottonwood Tree*   **Morton**
American, b. 1887   Oil on canvas   **Gallery**
O'Keeffe paints natural forms in a Precisionist style that has become increasingly abstract with passing years. She has worked mostly in the Southwest, which has a special attraction for her.

PABLO PICASSO   *Woman with Pitcher*   **Not on**
Spanish, 1881–1973   Pencil drawing   **Permanent**
Picasso was equally adept at depicting representational subjects or at executing **Exhibition** the more abstract styles he innovated or developed, at times working simultaneously with both.

Pablo Picasso, Woman with Pitcher. *Collection of the Santa Barbara Museum of Art, Santa Barbara, Wright Ludington*

Not on RICHARD DIEBENKORN *Woman with Checkerboard*
Permanent American, b. 1922 1956
Exhibition Oil on canvas
Shifting from still-life and figure painting to an abstract style, Diebenkorn returned to representation in the mid-1950s while continuing to favor color masses over line, lessons he learned from abstraction.

FACILITIES

Lectures on a variety of art-related subjects are offered.

Changing Exhibitions of a wide variety of works of art are regularly featured.

Films, both classic and on art, are screened. Call for program.

The *Art Rental Gallery* features the work of artists who have participated in the gallery during the past year.

Hours: Tuesday–Saturday, 11 A.M.–5 P.M.; Sunday, 12 P.M.–5 P.M. *Closed:* Mondays, holidays.

Admission: Free.

UNIVERSITY OF CALIFORNIA
SANTA BARBARA MUSEUM
Santa Barbara, CA 93106
Tel: (805)961-2951

The museum brings to the campus and the community a program of changing exhibits of painting, sculpture, printmaking, drawing, photography, ceramics, indigenous art and architecture. Some of these exhibitions are contemporary in nature, others are concerned with the history of art and the environment.

SAMPLING THE COLLECTION

Sedgwick *SEDGWICK COLLECTION*
Gallery
GIOVANNI BELLINI (?) *Madonna and Child*
Italian, Venetian, ca. 1430–1516 Oil on canvas
Bellini, a major influence on his contemporaries and on the following generation, was the most important of the Venetian *Madonnieri* (Madonna painters) bringing great imagination to these works.

JUAN DE FLANDES *Juana la Loca*
Flemish, fl. 1496–1519 Oil
Juan de Flandes was court painter to Isabella of Spain. The scope of his work was highly regarded in a country whose artists were still limited.

SCHOOL OF HUGO VAN DER
GOES *Adoration of the Magi*
Flemish, 15th c. Oil
Van der Goes was known for his dramatic works. They were often executed on a grand scale, which was unusual for a Flemish painter.

Gainey *MORGENROTH COLLECTION*
Gallery
ANTONIO PISANELLO *Domenico Malatesta Novello*
Italian, ca. 1395–1455 Bronze, reverse side only

Pisanello was best known as a portrait medalist, although he was an accomplished narrative painter as well.

CARADOSSO (CHRISTOFORO	
FOPPA)	*Lodovico Maria Sforza,*
Italian, ca. 1445–1526	*Il Moro*
	The Doge of Genoa (?)
	Bronze, reverse side

Caradosso was a renowned goldsmith, bronzeworker and sculptor. He was also much in demand by royalty for evaluating and procuring jewels and antique objects of art.

ARCHITECTURAL ARCHIVES

The archives contain drawings by many California-area architects, including R. M. Schindler, Irving S. Gill, Kem Weber, Gregory Ain, John Hudson Thomas, Myron Hunt, John Byers and Edla Muir.

FACILITIES

Tours, Lectures and *Gallery Talks* are offered.

Changing Exhibitions of the work of a variety of artists are a regular museum feature.

The *Sales Desk* sells catalogs published by the museum ranging in price from 25¢ to $8.50.

Hours: Tuesday–Saturday, 10 A.M.–4 P.M.; Sunday, holidays, 1 P.M.–5 P.M.
 Closed: Mondays, New Year's, Thanksgiving, Christmas.

Admission: Free.

SANTA CLARA

DE SAISSET ART GALLERY
University of Santa Clara
Santa Clara, CA 95053
Tel: (408)984-4528

This university museum has a continually expanding permanent collection, which includes American works from the early 19th century and European works from the early 18th century. In addition, there are African, Oriental, early California Mission, ivory, porcelain, silver, photography and graphic collections.

SAMPLING THE COLLECTION

GOBELINS MANUFACTORY	*2 Tapestries*	**Auditorium**
French	17th c.	
	Callio Dutch West Indies Series	

These tapestries were woven by Gobelins, one of the great tapestry houses of

France. In this period when the design was transferred to wool, details were commonly omitted.

Auditorium ANDRE-CHARLES BOULLE *Tall Case Clock*
French, 1642–1732 Black veneer wood with metal inlay and ormolu trim
Tall case clocks were important decorative furniture. Instruments of great precision, they were invented to protect the weights from interference. Boulle used marquetry in metal or tortoiseshell inlay.

Sculpture PIETRO CALVI *Othello*
Court, Italian, 1833–1884 Marble and bronze
Othello Calvi's sculptured busts appeared in many exhibits in this country and in Europe.
Gallery This one won the sculpture award at the Chicago World's Fair of 1893.

Downstairs, J. G. WAGNER *6 Portrait Plates*
Large Austrian, 18th c. Porcelain, semiprecious stones
Central The outer edges of these hand-painted portrait plates are set with garnet, car-
Display Case nelian, jade and turquoise. Wagner was a porcelain painter who worked at the Meissen factory from 1739.

Foyer Display EUROPEAN *Madonna Triptych*
Case early 18th c.
Ivory
The Madonna's skirt opens out to form a triptych with carvings of angels on either side. The center panel depicts a scene from the life of Christ.

California AMERICAN *Bishop's Chair*
Mission 19th c.
Room Mahogany, calf and cloth
This was the chair of Bishop Garcia Diego Marlinique, first Bishop of California from 1841 to 1846.

Downstairs, CHINESE *Man and Woman on Horseback*
Oriental Sui Dynasty, 581–618 *(Pair)*
Display Clay
Case Two examples of Ming Ch'i, or funerary statuary, which were buried with the dead.

FACILITIES

Tours of the gallery are conducted regularly for small or large groups.

Lectures on art and related subjects are given mostly in the evenings.

Changing Exhibitions of the work of a variety of artists is a regular museum feature.

A *Concert* series is offered.

The *Gallery Shop* features art reproduction cards, posters, antique objects d'art and memorabilia from the 1930s and 1940s. There is also jewelry from local craftsmen. Most items are under $15 although the prices range from 25¢ to $30. The shop is open Tuesday–Friday, 11 A.M.–3 P.M.; Saturday–Sunday, 1 P.M.–4 P.M.

Hours: Tuesday–Friday, 10 A.M.–5 P.M.; Saturday–Sunday, 1 P.M.–5 P.M. *Closed:* Mondays, August, national holidays, Good Friday, Martin Luther King, Jr.'s birthday.

Admission: Free, but donations are gratefully accepted.

STANFORD

STANFORD UNIVERSITY MUSEUM AND ART GALLERY
Museum Way
Stanford, CA 94305
Tel: (415)497-4177
Education Office
Tel: (415)497-3469

When the Stanford museum was opened to visitors in 1894, it was the largest private museum in the world. One of the earliest structures on the West Coast to be made of reinforced concrete, the central pavilion withstood the earthquake of 1906. The collections presently comprise Egyptian, Greek, and Roman art; African, pre-Columbian, Pacific Island and North American Indian art; Oriental and Indian paintings, sculpture, textiles, and decorative arts; European and American paintings, sculpture, prints, and drawings; photographs, including the Muybridge early motion studies; the B. Gerald Cantor Gallery of Rodin bronzes and Stanford family memorabilia.

SAMPLING THE COLLECTION

AMERICAN   *The Last Spike*   **1st Floor,**
Commemorating the first transcontinental railway, the golden spike was sym- **Stanford**
bolically driven into the tie uniting the Union Pacific and the California Pacific **Collection**
at Promontory, Utah, on May 10, 1869.

AUGUSTE RODIN   *Bronzes*   **1st Floor,**
French, 1840–1917   **Cantor**
Rodin, the most renowned 19th-century sculptor, produced such lifelike **Gallery**
bronzes that he was accused of molding them on living figures. Influenced by
Michelangelo, he created fragmentary sculpture, parts of bodies and unfinished
figures.

CHINESE   *Reclining Buddha in the*   **1st Floor**
Ming Dynasty, 1368–1644   *Attitude of Nirvana*
                                 Wood
The Ming Dynasty was the last period in which sculpture appeared on any grand
scale. During this time sculptors abandoned stone in favor of easier materials.

18TH-C. VENETIAN PAINTINGS AND DRAWINGS

FRANCESCO GUARDI   *Paintings and Drawings*   **1st Floor,**
Italian, 1712–1793   **European**
Famous for his views of Venice, Guardi with his gay palette and interest in light **Gallery**
was a precursor of the Impressionists.

GIOVANNI BATTISTA TIEPOLO   *Paintings and Drawings*   **1st Floor,**
Italian, 1696–1770   **European**
                                                                    Gallery
GIOVANNI DOMENICO TIEPOLO
Italian, 1727–1804
G. D. Tiepolo was chief assistant to his father, the most famed of the Rococo
decorative painters. Their work adorns many churches and palaces.

FRANK E. BUCK COLLECTION OF CHINESE JADE   **1st Floor**

Fifty-three pieces—carved from Imperial jade, lapis lazuli, rock crystal—include urns, vases, scrolls, incense burners, animals, dishes, boxes. The majority are from the Ch'ien Lung period (1736–1795) of the Ch'ing Dynasty (1644–1912), a time when craftsmen were encouraged and jade carvings reached a high level of decorative perfection. There are also items from the Sung (A.D. 960–1279) and Ming (1368–1644) dynasties.

FACILITIES

Guided Tours may be arranged through the Educational Curator's office.

Changing Exhibitions of the work of a variety of artists is a regular feature both of the museum and of its auxiliary, the Stanford Art Gallery.

The *Art Gallery Bookshop* sells books, note cards, calendars and other related materials.

Hours: Tuesday–Friday, 10 A.M–4:45 P.M.; Saturday–Sunday, 1 P.M.–4:45 P.M.
         Closed: Mondays, September, July 4, Christmas, New Year's.

Admission: Free.

STOCKTON

PIONEER MUSEUM AND HAGGIN GALLERIES
Victory Park
1201 North Pershing Ave.
Stockton, CA 95203
Tel: (209)462-4116

The three-story building houses art and history collections. The art collection is comprised mainly of 19th-century American and European paintings, while the history collection contains items on California arranged in interpretive display settings.

SAMPLING THE COLLECTION

MAJOR ART ITEMS

Rotunda   ALBERT BIERSTADT   *Sunset in Yosemite Valley*
              American, 1830–1902   1868
                                        Oil on canvas

Born in Germany and influenced by his early training there, Bierstadt gained immediate popularity in the United States because of his subject matter. The paintings are mostly of the American West.

                                        Looking up the Yosemite
                                        Valley
                                        1863
                                        Oil on canvas

Forceful lighting and a careful depiction of texture were characteristic of Bierstadt's work.

Haggin Room   ADOLPHE WILLIAM BOUGUEREAU   *Nymphs Bathing*
                  French, 1825–1905   1878
                                               Oil on canvas

Throughout his life Bouguereau was a very popular painter. His work was carefully executed and his canvases were often of sensuous mythological subjects.

ROSA BONHEUR French, 1822–1899	*Gathering for the Hunt* 1856 Oil on canvas	**Haggin Room**

Bonheur is known mostly for her animal paintings.

JEAN LEON GEROME French, 1824–1904	*The Artist and His Model* Oil on canvas	**McKee Room**

Gérôme's immensely popular paintings were Neoclassical and in direct opposition to the Impressionists. The great acceptance of his work was most likely due, in part, to its somewhat erotic quality.

MAJOR HISTORICAL ITEMS

AMERICAN California	*Old Betsy* 1861	**Vehicle** **Gallery**

The second oldest steam fire engine in the United States.

AMERICAN California	*Holt 75 Tractor* 1918	**Holt** **Memorial**

This track-type tractor is an extensively restored Stockton-built machine. **Hall**

AMERICAN California	*Portion of Machine Shop* *Building* ca. 1900	**Holt** **Memorial** **Hall**

This shop building is part of the experimental shop used by Stockton inventor Benjamin Holt.

AMERICAN California	*Herbalist's Equipment* Chinese 1900	**Storefront** **Gallery**

The fixtures and stock are from Stockton's Chinatown.

FACILITIES

Free Museum Tours for the general public each Saturday at 1:45 P.M. Special tours for children and adult groups are conducted by appointment Tuesday through Saturday.

Lecture, Concert and *Film Programs* are occasionally offered.

Changing Exhibitions of the work of a variety of artists is a regular museum feature.

Picnic Facilities are available in the park where the museum is situated.

Hours: Tuesday–Sunday, 1:30 P.M.-5 P.M. *Closed:* Mondays, New Year's, Christmas, Thanksgiving.

Admission: Free.

COLORADO

COLORADO SPRINGS

COLORADO SPRINGS FINE ART CENTER
30 West Dale St.
Colorado Springs, CO 80903
Tel: (303)634-5581

The first multipurpose fine arts center in the country includes the Taylor Museum, the Fine Arts Collection and the Bemis Art School for children. The museum's possessions are divided between the Fine Arts Collection which contains European, American and Oriental art and the Taylor Museum Collection which focuses on folk and native American art. The latter contains an adobe chapel with original pieces of artwork. It also houses the largest collection of santos (carvings of saints) in the Southwest.

SAMPLING THE COLLECTION

Fine Arts Collection	WALT KUHN American, 1880–1949	*Trio* 1937 Oil on canvas

Trio is an important work of Kuhn's as it is one of the few instances in which the artist treats his favorite subject, the clown, on a truly monumental scale.

Fine Arts Collection	ARTHUR G. DOVE American, 1880–1946	*Fog Horns* 1929 Oil on canvas

Dove, a pioneer of American abstraction, sought to capture the essential spirit of nature through his art. In *Fog Horns,* he uses color and abstract shapes to evoke the eerie sound of foghorns.

Taylor Museum Collection	ATT. TO J. RAPHAEL ARAGON Talpa, New Mexico	*Christ Crucified* 19th c. Polychromed wood

This bulto (sculpture) is carved in the simple style common to 19th-century New Mexico folk sculpture. The emotional work is typical of the art created by members of the Penitente Brotherhood.

Taylor Museum Collection	AMERICAN Navajo Indian	*Chief Blanket* ca. 1850 Wool with natural dyes

Representing one of the earliest styles in the development of Navajo weaving, this blanket is a fine example of Southwest Indian textiles.

FACILITIES

Lecture, Music, Dance and *Film* programs are all offered. Call for schedule information.

Exterior view. Courtesy Colorado Springs Fine Art Center, Colorado Springs

Temporary Exhibitions culled from the museum's collection or *Loan Exhibitions* from other institutions are regular features of the museum's program.

The *Library* is open Tuesday–Saturday, 10 A.M.–5 P.M.

The *Sales Shop's* most popular items are cards, books, museum replicas, papier-mâché boxes, Mexican wares, American Indian goods and children's gifts. The children's items range in price from 50¢ to $5, while adult material has a varied price range.

Hours: Tuesday, Thursday, 10 A.M.–9 P.M. Wednesday, Friday, Saturday, 10 A.M.–5 P.M.; Sunday, 1:30 P.M.–5 P.M. *Closed:* Mondays, New Year's, Thanksgiving, Christmas.

Admission: Free.

DENVER

DENVER ART MUSEUM
100 West 14th Ave. Parkway
Denver, CO 80204
Tel: (303)575-2793

Since 1971 the museum, which was founded in 1894, has been located in a unique six-story building of gray glass tile. The irregular window placement in its glimmering façade provides protection from direct sunlight for the delicate objects inside. Pairs of galleries are stacked vertically making them easily accessible. Each pair is connected by a service area and outdoor loges. The collection's strength is concentrated in American Indian art that displays many pieces in settings reflecting their original use; art of the Americas features pre-Columbian, Spanish Colonial and Southwestern art in environmental settings, a suite of rooms from a 1770 Rhode Island house and Western art; African, Oceanic and Northwest Coast art includes a two-story exhibit of totem poles; ancient Egyptian and European art contains a Kress collection of Renaissance art and English Tudor, Spanish Baroque and French Gothic rooms; Oriental art displays porcelains, bronzes, scrolls and stone figures. Textiles and costumes house an outstanding collection of quilts and coverlets.

SAMPLING THE COLLECTION

Bach Wing, Main Floor

CONTEMPORARY ART

WILLIAM T. WILEY
American, b. 1937

The Hound Harbor Series
(Four parts)
1977
Mixed media

Wiley, a prizewinning painter, who works in the San Francisco area, has also been a teacher.

FRANK STELLA
American, b. 1936

Warka I
1973
Mixed media construction collage

In the 1970s Stella created colorful shaped structures in geometric patterns. Although they are displayed on walls they can easily be confused with sculpture.

DONALD JUDD
American, b. 1928

Untitled
ca. 1970
Stainless steel cubes, 8 pieces,
(4'x4'x4')

Exterior view. Courtesy Denver Art Museum, Denver

Seeking perfect harmony by repeating identical objects, most often in series, Judd's Minimal sculpture does not invite the viewer to become part of it but rather holds him aloof from it.

AFRICAN ART

Mezzanine Level

OSAMUKA FOR OSI VILLAGE
Nigeria, Yoruba Tribe

Epa Headdress
ca. 1920
Carved wood

This headdress is worn during festivals commemorating Epa, a wood-carving deity. It is unusual because of its size and intricate carving.

THE MASTER OF IKARE
Nigeria, Yoruba Tribe

Carved Door
ca. 1978
Wood

The Master decorated a number of placards for Yoruba's kings, carving doors and pillars in intricate designs of high relief.

OCEANIC ART

Mezzanine Level

POLYNESIAN
Tonga

Carved Club
18th–19th c.
Wood

Polynesian carving exists mainly on useful articles, figurative sculpture being less common. Usually unpainted, they are simply shaped but intricately carved in small geometric patterns.

MELANESIAN   *Male Figure*
New Hebrides, Makekula   ca. 1900
                                    Carved wood and shell
A hierarchical men's society required numerous masks, figures and articles during ceremonial rites. The human figure, particularly the head, is the most popular theme of Melanesian art.

Mezzanine Level

NORTHWEST COAST ART

ALASKAN   *Interior House Screens*
Tlingit People   ca. 1825
                                    Painted cedar boards with raven
                                    design
Screens were used for house partitions as well as decoration. The raven motif is popular with Northwest Coast peoples.

2nd Floor

NATIVE AMERICAN ART

SIOUX INDIAN   *Beaded Buffalo Robe*
                                    mid-19th c.
Unusual because it was made for a woman and intricately beaded (in a box and border design) rather than painted, this robe's geometric design is thought to be symbolic of the buffalo.

3rd Floor

NEW WORLD SPANISH COLONIAL ART

DIEGO QUISPE TITO INGA   *Our Lady of the Victory of*
Peru, Cuzco, 17th c.   *Malaga*
                                    ca. 1640
                                    Oil on canvas
This devotion of the Virgin of Guadalupe, Caceres, Spain, lavishly illustrates the Virgin and Child in ornate Cuzco style elaborated with gold designs inspired by Spanish and Flemish engravings sent to Peru.

CIPRIANO GUTIERREZ   *Adoration of the Magi*
Peru, Cuzco, 18th c.   ca. 1735
                                    Oil on canvas
This copy of the Gothenberg *Adoration* by Rubens was derived from the Bolswert engraving of 1631. It was possibly the model for the painting above the Cuzco Cathedral's Triunfo church entrance.

SEBASTIAN SALCEDO   *Maria S.S. de Mexico*
Peru, Cuzco, 18th c.   1779
                                    Oil on copper panel
Exacting detail and monumental composition in small scale suggests this painting was a model for an enormous mural. It displays 58 figures about the vision of Guadalupe as she appeared in Mexico.

3rd Floor

PRE-COLUMBIAN ART

MEXICAN   *Seated Figure, the Zumpango Baby*
Guerrero, Zumpango Del Rio area,   Ceramic
Olmec Culture, Middle Preclassic
Period, ca. 1100–900 B.C.

Possibly the only large ceramic Olmec figure to survive unbroken. Its exceptional condition with traces of post fired paint suggests what colorful painted details such figures originally had before burial.

GUATEMALAN   *Wooden Lintel*
Central Peten, Mayan Culture,   Carved zapote wood, traces
Late Classic Period, ca. A.D. 650   of red paint
Possibly the oldest surviving Mayan wood lintel, the carved costume details and glyphic text is different from the other seven extant. It is tentatively dated nearly one hundred years earlier.

WEST COLOMBIAN   *Popayan Seated Figure,*
Cauca Valley, Popayan Culture,   *the Tower Warrior*
ca. A.D. 1000–1400   Ceramic with traces of polychrome
This hollow urn, the most complete surviving example of Popayan ceramics, portrays a warrior. An elaborate headdress is the lid. A fanciful animal on his back may represent his alter ego.

SANTERO ART OF THE SOUTHWEST   **3rd Floor**

PEDRO ANTONIO FRESQUIZ   *Altar Finial of the Holy Trinity*
New Mexico, San Juan Pueblo,   ca. 1820
19th c.   Pine panel, gesso and polychrome
                                   (retablo)
Panel painting is typical of Southwestern Santero art. This fragment from an original wooden altar screen depicts the Holy Trinity as three identical young men seated on imaginative clouds that resemble feathers.

SANTO NINO SANTERO   *Nazarene Christ Crucified*
New Mexico, Santa Cruz area,   ca. 1830
19th c.   Cottonwood root, cotton fabric,
                                   gesso and polychrome (bulto)
Thought to be the largest and most monumental surviving piece by the Santo Niño Santero, this nearly life-size corpus is well carved with natural rendering of the body details.

NEW MEXICAN   *Christ Flagellated*
Chimayo area   ca. 1820
                                   Cottonwood root, pine frame,
                                   leather, gesso and polychrome
                                   (bulto)
The hollow frame construction allowed this figure to be carried in Holy Week processions. The articulated arms could be tied to a column or carry a cross to enact Christ's passion.

AMERICAN ART   **3rd Floor**

THOMAS COLE   *Dream of Arcadia*
1801–1848   1837
                                   Oil on canvas
This is a fantasy landscape by one of the most important members of the Hudson River School of painting. Cole's early romantic style became broader as his imagination became freer.

ARTHUR FITZWILLIAM TAIT   *Trappers at Fault, Looking*
1819–1905   *for the Trail*
                                   1852
                                   Oil on canvas

The artist, like many Easterners, was fascinated with the opening of the West. This colorful scene illustrates his great attention to detail.

3rd Floor   WILLARD LEROY METCALF   *The Ten-Cent Breakfast*
1858–1925   1887
Oil on canvas
Metcalf's impressionistic painting is of special interest because it portrays a group of American artists and literary figures (including Robert Louis Stevenson) who studied in France before returning to America.

4th Floor   *EUROPEAN ART*

FRANCESCO PESELLINO   *Madonna and Child Before*
Italian, ca. 1422–1457   *a Marble Niche*
ca. 1450–1455
Oil on panel
The Madonna and Child were favorite subjects of Pesellino and he depicted them many times. The soft, supple modeling of his figures was accomplished in harmonious colors.

HILAIRE GERMAIN EDGAR DEGAS   *Examen de Danse (Danseuses*
French, 1834–1917   *à Leur Toilette)*
ca. 1880
Pastel on paper
Degas's powerful graphic style creates a lively tension between three-dimensional form and two-dimensional planes while probing his characters' psychological aspects, hinted at in the drama of this work.

PABLO PICASSO   *Paysage, Horta de Ebro*
Spanish, 1881–1973   1909
Oil on canvas
This painting was executed in the summer of 1909 when Picasso was beginning to crystallize his thoughts and expression on Analytical Cubism.

5th Floor   *ORIENTAL ART*

SOUTH INDIAN   *Shiva Natarāja*
13th c.
Bronze
The Hindu god, Shiva, as the cosmic dancer, embodies eternal energy while performing the dance of creation instilling life into the universe. The vigorous image, in perfectly balanced composition, vibrant yet motionless, symbolizes eternity.

CHINESE   *Kuan Yin Seated in Royal Ease*
10th c.
Polychromed wood
Kuan Yin, Buddhist deity of mercy, is elegantly seated in the pose of "royal ease." The image is imbued with a gentle, benign calm combined with a richness of dress.

COSTUMES AND TEXTILES

4th Floor,   FLEMISH   *Feast of the Passover*
French Gothic   16th c.
Room   Embroidered panel, gold thread on crimson velvet

Flemish tapestries and embroideries were demanded by emperors, kings and popes, as well as by the bourgeoisie, for decorative and commemorative purposes. History, religion, hunting and verdure designs were all popular subjects.

PERSIAN	*Two-Headed Eagle*	**5th Floor,**
Buyid Dynasty, 945–1055	Silk fragment	**Oriental**

This piece of silk is said to have come from the rock tombs in Rhages, once a **Art** Persian city.

JOSEP GRAU-GARRIGA	*Ecumenisme*	**6th Floor**
Spanish, b. 1929	1969–1970	
	Mixed media	

This piece has a strong feeling of the artist's first area of art, which was collage, and illustrates the imaginative work being done by artists today.

FACILITIES

Temporary Exhibitions culled from the museum's collection or *Loan Exhibitions* from other institutions are regular features of the museum's program.

The *Restaurant* serves meals. Wine and cocktails are available. A pleasantly shaded patio invites summer visitors. Open: Tuesday–Saturday, 11 A.M.–2:30 P.M.; Wednesday evening, 5:30 P.M.–7:30 P.M.

The *Book Shop* sells jewelry and art replicas as well as books, postcards and posters.

Free *Guided Tours* are available.

Wheelchairs and *Strollers* are available. The museum is also accessible to the handicapped.

Meet at Information Desk

Hours: Tuesday–Saturday, 9 A.M.–5 P.M.; Sunday, 1 P.M.–5 P.M.; Wednesday evenings until 9 P.M. *Closed:* Mondays, major holidays.

Admission: Free. There is occasionally a fee for special exhibitions.

HAWAII

HONOLULU

HONOLULU ACADEMY OF ARTS
900 South Beretania St.
Honolulu, Hawaii 96814
Tel: (808)538-3693

The academy, founded in 1927, is housed in a graceful former residence of stuccoed stone with a tile roof. Designed in Polynesian, Oriental and Occidental styles, many of the 30 exhibition galleries open onto landscaped courtyards. Tropical flora enhances the interior. The building faces Thomas Square which, along with the academy, are Registered National Historic Places. The museum is particularly celebrated for its Asian collection containing sculpture, paintings and scrolls, screens, lacquerware, porcelain, ceramics and furniture from India, China, Japan and Korea. Additionally, one may view Western Masters, Mediterranean antiquities, medieval religious art and the Kress Collection of Italian Renaissance paintings. The Ukiyo-e Center contains examples of Japanese prints and other Oriental art from the James A. Michener Collection. There is also art of the Pacific, Africa and the Americas. The Clare Boothe Luce Wing, from which the contemporary sculpture garden may be entered, opened in 1977 and displays contemporary paintings. In 1960, the three-story educational wing was erected to provide art classes for all ages.

SAMPLING THE COLLECTION

ASIAN ART

Gallery 14 SUZUKI KUTSU   *Flowering Plum and Camellia*
Japanese, 1795–1858   Ink and color on paper
Japanese pictures were normally painted on silk, or paper from the bark of Mulberry trees. India ink, in varied gradations, is first applied, after which color, usually an opaque gouache, is added.

Gallery 17 KOREAN   *Attendant at a Buddhist Altar*
Yi Dynasty, 1392–1910   18th–19th c.
                                 Polychromed wood
Buddhist art was introduced from India in the 4th century conforming to Korean cultural patterns and adopting Korean costumes and facial characteristics. The Yi Dynasty was repressive and male-oriented.

Gallery 18 TRADITIONALLY ATT. TO MA FEN *The Hundred Geese*
Chinese, fl. end of 11th c.   Ink on paper, hand scroll
Ma Fen was from a family of illustrious painters. He is known for his animal paintings, his most celebrated work being *The Hundred Geese.*

Gallery 18 CHINESE   *The Bodhisattva Avalokitesvara*
Yüan Dynasty, 1260–1368   *(Kuan Yin)*
                                 13th c.
                                 Wood with polychrome coloring

Courtyard. *Courtesy Honolulu Academy of Arts, Honolulu*

Kuan Yin was the Chinese god of mercy. This figure typifies the style of the times with its oval face, systematically designed hair and the fashion of its drapery folds.

INDIAN   *Ganesha*   **Gallery 21**
                                          10th c. pink sandstone
Ganesha, the fat, genial, elephant-headed god of good luck, is a popular deity appearing often in Hindu art.

WESTERN ART

EMILE ANTOINE BOURDELLE   *La Grande Penelope*   **Central**
French, 1861–1929   Bronze   **Court**
Bourdelle was deeply influenced by Rodin and his impressionistic approach to modeling. He later rejected this style to adopt a more classical one. His portrait busts are his best known works.

CLAUDE MONET   *Water Lilies*   **Gallery 1**
French, 1840–1926   Oil on canvas

Monet painted many subjects in series capturing each in a variety of atmospheric conditions at different hours of the day. *Water Lilies* was executed in his mature years in his own lush garden.

Gallery 4   FLEMISH   *Queen Semiramis with Attendants*
Flanders, Tournai   ca. 1480
                                 "Millesfleurs" tapestry, wool and
                                 silk

In Tournai, the government regulated the tapestry industry which was handled by a few merchant-manufacturers. The tapestries were monumental in style and grandeur.

Gallery 5   FRANCESCO GRANACCI   *The Adoration of the Child*
Italian, 1477–1543   ca. 1500
                                 Tempera on wood panel

Granacci, of the Florentine School, helped pave the way for 16th-century styles of painting. A friend of Michelangelo, he assisted briefly with the Sistine Chapel ceiling.

NICOLAS DE LARGILLIERE   *Portrait of Helene de Thorigny*
French, 1656–1746   Oil on canvas

BLIN DE FONTENAY
French, ca. 1654–1715

De Largillière was a popular portraitist of the prosperous middle class. His sitters were casually posed against landscape backgrounds. The flowers were executed by de Fontenay.

FACILITIES

Guided Tours of the permanent collection are available every Wednesday and Friday, 11 A.M.

Lectures on art and related topics are frequently offered.

Temporary Exhibitions culled from the academy's collection or *Loan Exhibitions* from other institutions are regular features of the academy's program.

Classic *Films* and those on art are regularly screened. A young people's series is featured on Saturdays at 10:15 A.M. Call for program information.

The *Library* maintains a lending collection.

The *Garden Café* offers gourmet sandwich luncheons in an attractive setting. Open Tuesday–Friday. Sittings at 11:45 A.M. and 1:30 P.M. Reservations are suggested. Call (808)531-8865.

The *Academy Shop* counts among its most popular items art books, the Q.L.P. Series, replicas of jewelry from other museums, Hawaiiana, prints, notepaper and postcards.

Hours: Tuesday–Saturday, 10 A.M.–4:30 P.M.; Sunday, 2 P.M.–5 P.M. *Closed:*
         Mondays, New Year's, July 4, Labor Day, Thanksgiving, Christmas.
Admission: Free.

IDAHO

BOISE

BOISE GALLERY OF ART
716 South Capitol Blvd.
Julia Davis Park
Boise, ID 83701
Tel: (208)345-8330

Idaho's only public art museum was founded in 1931. Located in a park setting, it is in close proximity to the Boise State Historical Society and the State Zoo. It was remodeled in 1974, and contains five galleries.

SAMPLING THE COLLECTION

ALBRECHT DURER
German, 1471–1528

Knight, Death and Devil
1513
Engraving on antique laid paper

Dürer is unsurpassed in his mastery of the woodcut and of copper engraving. He perfected these techniques and influenced all European art by elevating the standards of the graphic arts.

PETER MORAN
American, 1841–1914

The Downs
Oil on canvas

Moran, a landscapist, animal painter and etcher, eventually settled in the United States, where he traveled and painted many Western scenes.

Exterior view. Courtesy Boise Gallery of Art, Boise

EDWARD KIENHOLZ   *Silvertone 17" Portable*
American, b. 1927   *Television*
                                    Sculpture—1967
Kienholz depicts the American scene in tableaux that use gaudy and shabby
materials to replicate realistic objects.

BILLY APPLE   *Idaho Fries*
American, b. 1935   1968
                                   Bronze and neon
Apple turned from Pop Art to the creation of UFOs (unidentified fluorescent
objects), bending neon tubing into odd shapes filled with mixtures of gas, which
produce unusual colors.

FACILITIES

Guided Tours may be arranged by appointment.

Temporary Exhibitions culled from the art gallery's collection or *Loan Exhibitions* from other institutions are regular features of the art gallery's program.

Programs of *Films, Lectures, Concerts, Drama and Poetry* are offered on Wednesday evenings.

The *Library* contains art books, slides, museum catalogs and magazines.

The *Sales Shop* carries art books, reproductions, prints, cards, stationery, regional crafts and gifts, with most items under $50.

Hours: Tuesday–Friday, 10 A.M.–5 P.M.; Saturday, Sunday 12 P.M.–5 P.M.
          Closed: Mondays, Thanksgiving, Christmas, New Year's.

Admission: Free.

MONTANA

BROWNING

MUSEUM OF THE PLAINS INDIAN
U.S. 90 west of
Browning, MT 59417
Tel: (406)338-3911

Historic displays in the museum are devoted to the numerous art forms related to the social and ceremonial aspects of the tribal cultures of the region. A special gallery is devoted to a continuing series of exhibitions promoting works by contemporary Native American artists and craftsmen.

SAMPLING THE COLLECTION

HISTORIC COSTUMES

These 19th-century costumes are presented on life-size manikins that highlight the diversity of these decorated garments worn by men, women and children of the Northern Plains tribe.

Historic Costumes. *Courtesy U.S. Department of the Interior, Indian Arts and Crafts Board*

FACILITIES

The Indian Arts and Crafts Shop offers arts and crafts by tribes of the Northern Plains. Beadwork includes moccasins, Indian dance accessories as well as modern purses, cigarette, glasses and check cover cases, hat bands, hair ornaments and jewelry. Other fashion items include buckskin gloves, suede jackets and vests. Many additional products as well as paintings by Northern Plains Indian artists are offered ranging in price from a few dollars to several hundred.

Hours: *June–September:* Daily, 9 A.M.–5 P.M.; *October–May:* Monday–Friday, 10 A.M.–4:30 P.M. *Closed:* New Year's, Thanksgiving, Christmas.

Admission: Free.

GREAT FALLS

C. M. RUSSELL MUSEUM
1201 Fourth Ave. N.
Great Falls, MT 59401
Tel: (406)452-7369

The museum's gallery, erected in 1953, is located alongside Russell's home and log cabin studio. Russell was a painter and sculptor of Western and Indian life. During the summer months the museum is filled with his oils, watercolors, cartoons, models and working sketches. Along with the permanent collection, including works by C. M. Russell and other Western artists, traveling exhibits occupy the museum during the winter. The value of the collection is in its variety which shows all phases of Russell's work. Also on view are paintings of artists working in the same field.

SAMPLING THE COLLECTION

CHARLES MARION RUSSELL
American, 1864–1926

The Jerkline
1912
Oil

Attack on the Red River Cart
1903
Watercolor

Both these paintings were executed during the period thought to be Russell's best.

FACILITIES

The *Museum Shop* features Russell prints, framed or unframed, $1–$75, Indian beadwork, original art and bronzes.

Hours: *Summer:* Daily, 10 A.M.–5 P.M. *Closed:* Mondays from September 15 to May 15, New Year's, Thanksgiving, Christmas, Easter Sunday.

Admission: Family, $2; 1 person, $1, students, 50¢.

HELENA

MONTANA HISTORICAL SOCIETY
225 North Roberts
Helena, MT 59601
Tel: (406)449-2695

The society consists of three galleries devoted to the history and art of Montana. The first gallery exhibits *7 Frontiers*—dioramas and display cases from prehistoric times up to present industrial development. *Territory Junction,* the second gallery, is a reconstruction of an 1880s town. The Mackay and Poindexter galleries present art from early Western days to the present.

Interior Gallery . *Courtesy Montana Historical Society, Helena*

SAMPLING THE COLLECTION

Mackay Gallery, Main Floor

CHARLES M. RUSSELL ARTWORK

Russell (1864–1926) delighted in painting and modeling Western and Indian themes. His oils, watercolors and sculpture are on view here and a gallery-within-a-gallery arrangement permits a display of photographs and memorabilia that give the viewer an intimate impression of the artist.

FACILITIES

A *Tour Train Ride* to historic sites around the city of Helena is available during the summer.

The *Sales Desk* offers reproductions of Charles Russell's artwork and a large selection of Western books are popular items. The prices range from 25¢ to $40.

Hours: *Summer:* Daily, 8 A.M.–8 P.M.; *Winter:* Weekdays, 8 A.M.–5 P.M.; weekends, 12 P.M.–5 P.M..

Admission: Free.

NEVADA

RENO

SIERRA NEVADA MUSEUM OF ART
549 Court St.
Reno, NV 89501
Tel: (702)329-3333

The museum, founded in 1931, is housed in a Georgian-style mansion of Historic Landmark status overlooking the Truckee River. The collection consists of paintings by Great Basin artists; prints dating from the 16th century, including works by Jacques Callot (1592–1635), Honoré Daumier (1808–1879), Otto Dix (1891–1969) and Diego Rivera (1886–1957); medieval manuscripts; early printed pages; Islamic carpets and Indian baskets.

SAMPLING THE COLLECTION

THOMAS MORAN   *Untitled Etching*
American, 1837–1926   ca. 1885–1890
Moran was a painter and printmaker who first concentrated on Hudson River landscapes. He later traveled to the West, where he recorded the scenery and enjoyed great popular acclaim.

MAYNARD DIXON   *Edge of the Amargosa Desert*
American, 1875–1946   1927
                                Oil
Dixon was an artist who lived and worked in northern Nevada.

FACILITIES

Changing Exhibitions are regularly featured.

The *Museum School* offers regular classes in all aspects of the fine arts and art appreciation. $33 for members.

The *Museum Shop* stocks books, cards, paper and many hard-to-find special gifts.

Hours: Tuesday–Saturday, 10 A.M.–4 P.M.; Sunday, 12 P.M.–4 P.M. *Closed:* Mondays, most holidays.

Admission: Voluntary donation.

NEW MEXICO

ALBUQUERQUE

ART MUSEUM, UNIVERSITY OF NEW MEXICO
Fine Arts Center
Albuquerque, NM 87131
Tel: (505)277-4001

Playing host to ever-increasing numbers of spectators, this university museum's permanent collection includes more than 2,500 paintings, drawings, prints, photographs, sculpture and art objects. Areas of particular interest are 20th-century American art with some emphasis on artists who have worked in New Mexico; the history of photography, presenting more than 400 daguerreotypes, ambrotypes and tintypes; and a broad print collection concentrating on the history of 19th- and 20th-century lithographs.

SAMPLING THE COLLECTION

RICHARD DIEBENKORN   *Untitled (Albuquerque, 1951)*
American, b. 1922   1951
                            Oil on canvas
This painting was part of Diebenkorn's Master's Thesis show. His expressionistic style with energetic calligraphic line was freer than his earlier work.

GASTON LACHAISE   *Torso*
French-American, 1882–1935 1927
                            Bronze
This larger than life-size figure, one of Lachaise's major works, illustrates the artist's lifelong celebration of the female nude.

GEORGIA O'KEEFFE   *Tent Door at Night*
American, b. 1887   ca. 1913
                            Watercolor
A significant early work, this clearly indicates O'Keeffe's remarkable venturesomeness even at an early stage in her development.

THEOPHILE STEINLEN   *La Rue*
Swiss/French, 1859–1923   1896
                            Lithograph
One of the largest known 19th-century posters, this monumental work reveals Steinlen's preoccupation with the working classes.

ALFRED STIEGLITZ   *Flatiron Building*
American, 1864–1946   ca. 1903
                            Photograph
An example of Stieglitz's early photographs of New York City, this is one of the few silver prints known to exist of this photograph.

FACILITIES

Guided Tours, Lectures and *Gallery Talks* are offered. Call for schedule information.

Changing Exhibitions are regularly featured.

The *Sales Desk* sells unusual art books and exhibition catalogs.

Hours: Tuesday–Friday, 10 A.M.–5 P.M.; Sunday, 1 P.M.–5 P.M. *Closed:* Mondays, Saturdays, August, national holidays.

Admission: 50¢ per person; no charge for students.

ROSWELL

ROSWELL MUSEUM AND ART CENTER
100 West 11th St.
Roswell, NM 88201
Tel: (505)622-4700

The original one-gallery structure and furnishings were built by WPA craftsmen. Today the museum has eleven galleries visited by over 50,000 people annually. Its permanent collections include the Southwestern Art collection representing not only established painters but younger, experimental artists as well. The Peter Hurd collection contains the largest number of this regional artist's work in the world. The Witter Bynner collection is a highly personal selection of Chinese art.

SAMPLING THE COLLECTION

GEORGIA O'KEEFFE
American, b. 1887

Ram's Skull with Brown Leaves
1936
Oil on canvas

An example of O'Keeffe's Abstract Precisionist style, this painting displays her lively fascination with the formal aspects of the skull.

PETER HURD
American, b. 1904

The Gate and Beyond
1952
Egg tempera on masonite

Northeast Galleries

Hurd is a tempera painter of mostly Western themes. This landscape conveys the sense of vast spaces, intense light and distant mountains that are familiar aspects of Southwestern scenery.

HANK JENSEN
American, b. 1930

Chicago Piano
1972
Fiberglass-faced plywood

In Front of Museum Entrance

Colored brilliant rust red, this aggressive sculpture with its skyward tilted limbs makes playful allusion to the history behind its title.

LUIS JIMENEZ
American, b. 1940

The End of the Trail with Electric Sunset
1974
Fiberglass resin-polychrome

Anderson Gallery

This contemporary treatment of a well-known theme from the myth of the great West and the noble savage is created with modern color and material. The sculpture's effect is both tragic and comic.

ROBERT H. GODDARD WORKSHOP
Rocket research inventor Goddard's shop includes tools and machinery from the twelve-year period of his Roswell residency.

FACILITIES

Changing Exhibitions are regularly featured.

At Entrance   The *Gift Shop* carries Indian artifacts such as pottery, small rugs and baskets. There are also patio bells, small sand paintings, reproductions of Peter Hurd's work and paperback books on Southwestern subjects.

Hours: Daily, 9 A.M.–5 P.M.; Sundays, holidays, 1 P.M.–5 P.M. *Closed:* New Year's, Christmas.

Admission: Free.

SANTA FE

INSTITUTE OF AMERICAN INDIAN ARTS MUSEUM
Cerrillos Rd.
Santa Fe, NM 87501
Tel: (505)988-6281

The museum is part of an educational institution for young American Indians. It seeks ways to use the arts to remember the past while extending the Indian tradition into the future.

SAMPLING THE COLLECTION

HONORS COLLECTION
Approximately 12,000 items comprise this collection of arts and crafts executed by the Native Americans who have attended the institution since its inception.

ETHNOGRAPHIC COLLECTION
Roughly 3,000 items make up this collection of prehistoric and historic Native American paintings, sculpture, ceramics, beadwork, textiles, jewelry and miscellaneous pieces.

FACILITIES

Sales Shows are held from the first weekend in December to the second week of January. Also the second week of April to May 1. The students' works are for sale and are priced from $5 to $500.

Hours: *Winter:* Monday–Friday, 9 A.M.–5 P.M. *Closed weekends. Summer:* Monday–Saturday, 9 A.M.–5 P.M.; Sunday, 1 P.M.–5 P.M.

Admission: Free.

LABORATORY OF ANTHROPOLOGY
Old Santa Fe Trail
Santa Fe, NM 87503
Tel: (505)827-3241

Opened in 1931 as a private research center, the laboratory was given to the state in 1949. One function is to acquire, preserve and document anthropological collections belonging to the state. Included are 44,500 cataloged artifacts, both prehistoric and those from the beginning of recorded history. The laboratory also cares for more than 3,100 lots of bulk archeological collections unearthed through excavations dating back to about 1910. Among the material is Pueblo Indian pottery dating from the first half of the 19th century to the present. Basketry, jewelry, embroidery, sashes and other textiles from the same period are maintained, along with some of these same items from prehistoric times. Information is documented for each artifact such as what, when and how it was made and what it was used for.

FACILITIES

The *Library* houses books and periodicals relating to archeology and ethnology of New Mexico and the Southwest. It contains maps, rare books and the U.S. Geographic Survey. It also has books on climatology, geology and related scientific fields.

Hours: Monday–Friday, 8 A.M.–12 P.M.; 1 P.M.–5 P.M. *Closed:* Weekends, legal holidays.

Admission: Free.

MUSEUM OF FINE ARTS
On the Plaza
Santa Fe, NM 87503
Tel: (505)827-2351

Since its opening in 1917, the museum has been a major influence in the development of the arts in New Mexico. A classic example of pueblo architecture, it resembles certain historic mission churches. It houses 3,800 works of art: paintings, photographs, drawings, prints and sculptures.

SAMPLING THE COLLECTION

The following works may not always be on view.

ROBERT HENRI
American, 1865–1929

*Dieguito Roybal, the
Drummer of the Eagle Dance,
San Ildefonso*
ca. 1917
Oil on canvas

Henri, a painter and teacher, broke with academic tradition by encouraging his pupils to portray contemporary American life. He executed mostly commissioned portraits turning later to studies of people of varied backgrounds, calling them "my people."

BERT G. PHILLIPS
American, 1868–1956

*The Three Musicians of
the Baile*
ca. 1917
Oil on canvas

Exterior view. Courtesy Museum of Fine Arts, Sante Fe

This romantic view of Spanish culture is typical of the work of early painters in the Southwest.

JOHN SLOAN   *Music in the Plaza*
American, 1871–1951   1920
                                                    Oil on canvas
Sloan, an important teacher and influence on 20th-century art, abandoned European traditions. Early works of city themes, executed in gray tones, were replaced by a wider variety of subjects and a brighter palette.

FRITZ SCHOLDER   *Super Indian*
American, b. 1937   ca. 1970
                                                    Oil on canvas
Scholder, one of the foremost contemporary Indian painters, was influenced by the British artist, Francis Bacon. His international style is based on Pop Art with some protest about American Indians.

FACILITIES

Changing Exhibitions feature artists of New Mexico. The shows range from traditional art to contemporary lithographs and photographs.

The *Library* contains art books, periodicals, biographical files of artists represented in the permanent collection and catalogs of exhibits since 1917.

Special Events are featured such as theatrical productions and orchestral and choral groups.

The *Museum Shop* sells Southwestern Indian handcrafts (basketry, jewelry, leather goods), books of the region and prints of Southwestern artists.

Hours: Daily, 9 A.M.–4:45 P.M.   *Closed:* Mondays, mid-October to mid-March, Christmas, New Year's, July 4, Memorial Day, Labor Day, Columbus Day, Thanksgiving, Veterans Day.

Admission: Free.

MUSEUM OF INTERNATIONAL FOLK ART
A DIVISION OF THE MUSEUM OF NEW MEXICO
706 Camino Lejo
Santa Fe, NM 87501
Tel: (505)827-2544

Located on gently rolling land two miles south of Santa Fe's historic downtown plaza, the museum, opened in 1953, was designed to harmonize with the surrounding terrain. The collection increases constantly and, since the addition of the Girard Foundation collection, numbers about 134,000 objects. "The collections cut across boundaries of time and geography, presenting very personal glimpses of how artistic expressions have developed among widely divergent cultures, often with striking similarities." The museum's strength lies in its collection of folk costumes, tin-glazed pottery, textiles, Spanish Colonial household goods and Alpine art. The Girard Foundation collection includes toys, games, dolls, puzzles, ceramic figurines, puppets, Christmas decorations and other unique items from around the globe.

FACILITIES

Changing Exhibitions are regularly featured.

The *Museum Library,* open weekdays to researchers for on-premises study, contains books and periodicals on folk arts and crafts, folklore and folklife. It

Exterior view. Courtesy Museum of International Folk Art, Sante Fe

has slides and photographs of previous exhibitions and recordings and tran-
scripts of Spanish colonial folk literature and music.

The *Museum Shop,* though small, offers folk art from around the world, with
an emphasis on Mexican work. The most popular items are jewelry and bread
dough figures. Most items are under $20 but some cost up to $200.

Hours: Daily, 9 A.M.–4:45 P.M. *Winter months:* Closed Mondays. *Closed:*
          Thanksgiving, Christmas, July 4, Labor Day, Memorial Day, Columbus
          Day, Veterans Day, January 1.

Admission: Free.

WHEELWRIGHT MUSEUM
704 Camino Lejo
Santa Fe, NM 87501
Tel: (505)982-4636

When the Wheelwright changed its name in 1977 from the Museum of Navajo
Ceremonial Art, it sought also to change its image. Founded in 1937 as a
repository for art and religious artifacts, the heritage of the past of Navajo and
neighboring groups, it now includes work by contemporary artists providing
examples of an ever-changing Navajo culture. The permanent collection houses
over 25,000 items in the lower gallery in the building designed as a Navajo
hogan. It features sand paintings, tapestries, transitional textiles and old pawn
jewelry.

SAMPLING THE COLLECTION

NAVAJO   *Bridle*
                                    ca. 1900
                                    Silver mounted
During the 19th century the Navajos learned silversmithing from the Mexicans.
Bridle ornaments were made from hammered coins or cast from molten metal
in sandstone molds. Designs are not symbolic.

WOVEN BY NIECES OF
HOSTEEN KLAH (MEDICINE MAN),
NAVAJO   *Mother Earth and Father Sky*
                                    1930
                                    Wool blanket
In the last century women wove hand-spun wool into shawls and blankets of
simply striped patterns in perfect symmetry. Eventually elaborate patterns were
introduced with modern motifs appearing.

FACILITIES

Changing Exhibitions focus on aspects of Native American cultures in transition.

The *Case Trading Post* is a replica of a turn of the century Navajo trading post.
The most popular items on sale are Navajo rugs, Pueblo pottery and Navajo and
Pueblo jewelry priced from $10 to $3,000. Postcards, books, posters and fine
Southwest Indian art are also offered for sale.

Hours: Monday–Saturday, 10 A.M.–5 P.M. *Labor Day–Memorial Day:* Tues-
          day–Saturday, 10 A.M.–5 P.M.; Sunday 2 P.M.–5 P.M.

Admission: Suggested donation—adults, $1; children, 50¢.

OKLAHOMA

ANDARKO

SOUTHERN PLAINS INDIAN MUSEUM
U.S. 62 east of
Andarko, OK 73005
Tel: (405)247-6221

Historic displays in the museum are devoted to the numerous art forms related to the social and ceremonial aspects of the tribal cultures of the region. A special gallery houses a continuing series of exhibitions promoting works by contemporary Native American artists and craftsmen.

SAMPLING THE COLLECTION

SOUTHERN CHEYENNE   *Tipi Lining*
                          19th c.
                          Earth pigments on bison hide
This lining illustrates the daring and valorous exploits of Chief Red Bird, a Southern Cheyenne. Linings were hung in the tipi as protection from drafts and morning dew.

FACILITIES

The *Indian Arts and Crafts Shop* offers beadwork, featherwork and metalwork created in nickel silver, commonly referred to as "German silver-jewelry." There are also suede handbags, coin purses, glass cases and belts, all beaded. Many other items, including paintings by Native American artists, make this an interesting shop. Prices range from a few dollars to several hundred.

Hours: *June–September:* Monday–Saturday, 9 A.M.–5 P.M.; Sunday 1 P.M.–5 P.M. *October–May:* Tuesday–Saturday, 9 A.M.–5 P.M.; Sunday 1 P.M.–5 P.M. *Closed:* New Year's, Thanksgiving, Christmas.

Admission: Free.

BARTLESVILLE

WOOLAROC MUSEUM
State Highway 123
Bartlesville, OK 74003
Tel: (918)336-6747

The museum stands in a wildlife preserve of 3,500 acres used as hunting grounds by Plains Indians and traveled by early explorers. In the 1920s Frank Phillips established a home (The Lodge) and the museum. The museum contains paintings, sculpture and artifacts from prehistoric civilization in Oklahoma and from many Indian cultures, pioneers, cowboys, early statesmen and leaders. Also on view is a collection of Colt-Paterson guns. The exhibits in the National Y-Indian Guide Center animate and amplify the themes and treasures of the museum, lodge and wildlife preserve.

SAMPLING THE COLLECTION

Room 3,
East Wall

FRANK TENNEY JOHNSON
American, 1874–1939

Destiny
1936
Oil on canvas

Johnson painted vast canvases of cowboy and Indian scenes. He strove to depict costumes and flora accurately. Paintings of twilight, night scenes and thunderstorms show his interest in atmospheric effects.

Room 5,
North Wall

CHARLES MARION RUSSELL
American, 1864–1926

When Meat Was Plenty
1915
Oil on canvas

Russell delighted in the painting and sculpture of Western and Indian themes. His brilliantly colored paintings are filled with action.

Room 5,
East Wall

FREDERIC REMINGTON
American, 1861–1909

The Last Stand
1890
Oil on canvas

Remington's accurate but emotional renditions of Western and Indian life were extremely popular.

Room 5,
East Wall

WILLIAM R. LEIGH
American, 1866–1955

Visions of Yesterday
1943
Oil on canvas

Leigh's dramatic paintings are done with great anatomical detail. He traveled through the West sketching that place and time in history with great authenticity.

FACILITIES

Guided Tours may be arranged for organized groups.

Arrows Skyward is a multimedia program shown several times each day at the National Y-Indian Guide Center.

The *Concession Stand* sells barbecued buffalo sandwiches and Indian bread. Machines dispense soft drinks, coffee, candy, etc.

The *Museum Shop* carries postcards and guidebooks, Navajo and Zuñi jewelry (turquoise and silver) and books.

The *Guide Center Shop* caters to children and is priced accordingly.

Wheelchairs and *Strollers* are available for a small rental fee at the Guide Center.

Hours: Daily, 10 A.M.–5 P.M. *Closed:* Mondays, November 1–March 31, Thanksgiving, Christmas.

Admission: Free.

MUSKOGEE

FIVE CIVILIZED TRIBES MUSEUM
Agency Hill, Honor Heights Dr.
Muskogee, OK 74401
Tel: (918)693-1701

The museum was established in 1966 in the original Union Indian Agency building. It was erected in 1875 by the government to consolidate the affairs of the five Indian nations forced to leave their Southeastern homelands for Oklahoma. The museum aims to preserve and promote interest in the traditions, histories and cultures of the Creek, Cherokee, Seminole, Choctaw and Chickasaw. The collection includes paintings, wood carvings and sculptures. Display cases also exhibit clothing worn by students at the government school, examples of weapons used during the Civil War by the Five Tribes soldiers, cattle brands and barbed wire used on Indian ranches.

SAMPLING THE COLLECTION

JEROME TIGER PAINTINGS AND SCULPTURE   **Upstairs**
                                                           Gallery
Tiger, a Creek-Seminole, 1941–1967, was a prolific artist in his brief lifetime.

FACILITIES

The *Reference Library* is devoted exclusively to material on the Five Civilized Tribes.

The *Trading Post* is an interesting shop. All of the merchandise is created by Five Tribes artists. Some of the more popular items are beadwork, including necklaces, hair ties and rings from about $3; some fine jewelry of silver and of stones native to Oklahoma; scarves with designs of Indian cattle brands, $7; Five Civilized Tribes dictionaries from $5 to $10.50; hand-carved cotton stone book ends, $15 pair; baskets, $5–$20; and for children, leather headbands, $1.50, tomahawks, $1.50 and rawhide drums, $2.25 and $3.25. Prices are subject to change.

Hours: Monday–Saturday, 10 A.M.–5 P.M.; Sunday, 1 P.M.–5 P.M. *Closed:* Christmas.

Admission: Adults, 50¢; students, 25¢. Special group rates for 10 or more.

OKLAHOMA CITY

OKLAHOMA ART CENTER
Fair Park
3113 Pershing Blvd.
Oklahoma City, OK 73107
Tel: (405)946-4477

The center, established in 1946, is located on the state fairgrounds. It is a one-level structure of circular configuration built around a central sculpture court and pool. Two main galleries house the collection of American paintings; sculpture; prints; early American glass; graphics; drawings; and decorative art. The adjacent Arts Annex building offers educational and leisure time activities.

SAMPLING THE COLLECTION

THOMAS MORAN   *Falls of Toltec Gorge*
American, 1837–1926   1913
                                Oil

Moran was a member of the second generation of Hudson River painters. His enormous landscapes were much in demand during his lifetime.

BENJAMIN WEST   *Susanna Montgomery Wildey*
American, 1738–1820   *and Child*
                                1759
                                Oil

This portrait was executed very early in West's career, before he quit America for England. Largely self-taught, he established himself in Philadelphia painting commissioned portraits.

CHARLES BURCHFIELD   *Autumn Sunlight Filtering*
American, 1893–1967   *into the Woods*
                                1948
                                Watercolor

At this time Burchfield painted many scenes from nature in the same sinister, gloomy fashion that he used to depict the grim, small, Midwestern towns in his earlier work.

RICHARD ANUSKIEWICZ   *Diamond Chorma*
American, b. 1930   Serigraph

Anuskiewicz executes paintings and prints that are geometrically designed in distinct colors. He uses perspective to create stunning visual effects.

FACILITIES

Guided Tours are available.

Guided Tours for handicapped adults and young people are offered.

Temporary Exhibitions culled from the center's collection or *Loan Exhibitions* from other institutions are regular features of the center's program.

Conversations with Artists are scheduled on certain Sundays at 2:30. They bring the artist into direct contact with the public for questions and demonstrations.

The *Young People's Gallery* is a "hands on" participation area for young gallery visitors and their parents.

The *Bookstore* features fine books, $3–$50, stationery, posters, art games, puzzles and cards.

Artsplace II at 115 Park Avenue in downtown Oklahoma City offers *Monthly Exhibitions, Weekly Demonstrations* and *Films* (at noon), an extension of the OAC *Bookstore* and a *Sales and Rental Gallery* that carries original paintings, sculpture, jewelry, weavings and pottery. There are also authentic antique

Egyptian pieces and Alva museum replicas, original graphics and a few reproductions. There is a fine selection of Indian arts and crafts. Prices in the gallery
start at $7 and reach $3,000. Artsplace Hours: Monday–Friday, 10 A.M.–4 P.M.

Hours: Tuesday–Saturday, 10 A.M.–5 P.M.; Sunday, 1 P.M.–5 P.M.; *Closed:*
        Mondays, New Year's, Memorial Day, July 4, Thanksgiving, Christ-
        mas.

Admission: Over 17, $1; under 17, free. Special rates for prearranged tours
            of 15 or more. Call Education Department.

OKLAHOMA MUSEUM OF ART
7316 Nichols Rd.
Oklahoma City, OK 73120
Tel: (405)840-2759

The museum, founded in 1960, is presently housed in one of the last "grand
manner" mansions built in America before World War II. It is a fine example
of the late Academic Revival style of American 20th-century architecture. The
two-story limestone structure is situated in a 5-½-acre landscaped park featuring carved marble fountains and a large reflecting pool. The collection includes
works by major and minor Masters from the 17th through the 20th centuries
and also contains paintings, tapestries, furniture, porcelain, prints and drawings.
The museum stresses traditional values in art believing that they provide the
soundest basis for continuing artistic expression and offer a stability against
which the merits of contemporary art can be weighed. To this end, it exhibits
a wide range of art in historic and modern idioms.

SAMPLING THE COLLECTION

THOMAS HART BENTON   *Bathers*
American, 1889–1975   ca. 1918
                            Watercolors
Painted in Cubist and Synchromist styles, this painting was used as a study for
People of Chilmark, which is now in the Hirshhorn Museum in Washington,
D.C.

MARCELLUS COFFERMANS   *Coronation of the Virgin*   **2nd Floor,**
Flemish, act. 1549–1575   1562   **Gallery A**
                            Oil on copper panel
This small altarpiece was probably once in a private devotional chapel. Elabo-
rately framed, it is a typical example of the Northern European Mannerist style.

GUSTAVE COURBET   *Gorge in the Forest*   **2nd Floor,**
French, 1819–1877   ca. 1865   **Gallery D**
                            Oil on canvas
Courbet abandoned his early romantic style for a naturalistic one marked by
chiaroscuro and the use of heavy impasto.

THOMAS LAWRENCE   *Portrait of Baron Bexley*   **2nd Floor,**
British, 1769–1830   1824   **Gallery D**
                            Oil on canvas
Lawrence, a highly acclaimed portrait painter, was commissioned by George
IV to immortalize those who fought Napoleon. Two smaller versions of Baron
Bexley, Chancellor of the Exchequer, exist.

2nd Floor,	EUGENE LOUIS BOUDIN	*The Harbor at Portrieux,*
Gallery D	French, 1824–1898	*Low Tide*

1873
Oil on canvas

Boudin, who was born on the coast of Normandy, painted harbor and marine scenes in an atmospheric style which influenced the Impressionists, notably Monet.

FACILITIES

A variety of *Lectures, Concerts* and other programs are held throughout the year.

Changing Exhibitions are mounted each month, numbering about 48 each year.

Main Floor,
East End
The *Museum Shop* sells postcards, small art books, Alva museum reproductions, original jewelry and boutique-type items. Prices range from $5 to $150.

2nd Floor,
East End
The *Sales-Rental Gallery* presents work of the artist-members of the museum with selections changed each month. All media are offered.

Hours: Tuesday–Saturday, 10 A.M.–5 P.M.; Sunday, 1 P.M.–5 P.M.. *Closed:* Mondays, major holidays.

Admission: Adults, $1; those under 18 are free.

PONCA CITY

PONCA CITY INDIAN MUSEUM AND CULTURAL CENTER
1000 East Grand Ave.
Ponca City, OK 74601
Tel: (405)765-6108

The Cultural Center Museum was erected in 1914–1916 as the first mansion of E. W. Marland, oilman, philanthropist and tenth governor of Oklahoma. This showplace home contains 22 rooms spread over four floors. Because of its hanging staircase and other architectural features it has been listed on the National Register of Historic Places. The Cultural Center Museum includes the Indian Museum, which emphasizes material from five neighboring tribes: Ponca, Kaw, Otoe, Osage and Tonkawa; the 101 Ranch Room, containing memorabilia from the Miller Brothers 101 Ranch south of Ponca City in operation in the early 1900s; and the Bryant Baker Studio, a re-creation of the New York studio of the sculptor Bryant Baker, who was commissioned in 1927 by E. W. Marland to create the Pioneer Woman statue, a local landmark.

SAMPLING THE COLLECTION

Indian
Museum
RELICS FROM FERNANDINA

These artifacts are from Fernandina, an early French-Indian trading post, said to be the first white settlement in Oklahoma.

KACHINAS, BASKETS AND POTTERY

Kachinas are miniature carved dolls, male performers in painted mask and
decorated costume. Each doll represents one of 350 supernatural beings responsible for a variety of religious and social activities.

FACILITIES

Guided Tours for school classes are available with two-week reservations.

The *Museum Gift Shop* sells locally made Native American arts and crafts,
historical books, calendars and postcards.

Hours: Monday, Wednesday, Thursday, Friday, Saturday, 10 A.M.–5 P.M.;
        Sunday, 1 P.M.–5 P.M. *Closed:* Tuesdays, Christmas Eve, Christmas
        Day, New Year's Eve, New Year's Day.

Admission: Free.

TULSA

PHILBROOK ART CENTER
2727 South Rockford Rd.
Tulsa, OK 74152
Tel: (918)749-7941

The center, an Italian Renaissance-style villa, opened in 1939, is set amid 23
landscaped acres. It was once a private home. White exterior walls of stucco
and ground marble enclose the central Great Hall housing four columns recall-
ing those designed in the 17th century by Gianlorenzo Bernini for the Baldic-
chino at St. Peter's in Rome. The Great Hall, staircases, library, music room and
the formal dining room—now the Italian room, although somewhat altered—
retain their original flavor. Appropriate to the villa are the authentic Italian
Renaissance gardens that descend harmoniously from the East Terrace to a
series of reflecting pools, a swimming pool and a Classical *tempiétto*, a small
temple (under which were once dressing rooms for bathers). The museum
contains the American Indian collection, including some particularly fine American Indian paintings; American Indian baskets and pottery; the Kress Collection
of Italian Renaissance paintings and sculpture; African primitive sculpture;
American Indian costumes and artifacts; Chinese, Egyptian, Mesopotamian,
Greek and Roman art; European and American art and paintings of the oil
industry. Because the collection numbers too many articles to be displayed at
one time many items are subject to rotation.

SAMPLING THE COLLECTION

BIAGIO DI ANTONIO DA FIRENZE *Adoration of the Child with* **Main Floor,**
Italian, Florentine, ca. 1440–1504 *Saints and Donors* **Kress**
  Egg tempera on panel **Collection**

Experimentation with perspective and a sculptural style prevailed in 15th-cen-
tury Florentine painting. Stimulated by work being done on their cathedral, the
Florentine passion for solidity and relief found satisfaction in this style.

Main Floor, 19th-c. Gallery	ARTHUR FITZWILLIAM TAIT British/American, 1819–1905	*Trapper Looking Out* 1853 Oil on canvas

Tait, best known for his realistic paintings of rugged outdoor life, captures a dramatic moment in this scene. His paintings were often published by Currier and Ives.

Main Floor, Gillert Collection	THAI Sawankalok	*Elephant with Riders* 15th c. Ceramic

In the 12th century, kilns were established near the Luang River, an area offering high quality clay. Chinese tribes settling here brought with them ceramic techniques from China.

Ground Floor, American Indian Art	BLACKBEAR BOSIN American Indian	*Prairie Fire* Oil

This is the showpiece of the collection of contemporary American Indian paintings collected over 33 years of the *Annual American Indian Artists Exhibition,* a juried show.

Ground Floor, Field Collection	DATSOLALEE Washoe, Nevada, American Indian, 1831–1926	*Ceremonial Basket* 1918 Mountain willow, Nevada redbud, bracken root

Datsolalee, one of the few Indian women renowned for her excellent work, created baskets in difficult shapes naming them according to the pattern. Varicolored stitching material served as decoration.

FACILITIES

Philbrook Auditorium	*Lectures* and *Colloquia* where visitors may participate in lively interaction with guest speakers from around the world are often arranged.
Philbrook Auditorium	*Chamber Concerts* are offered throughout the year.
Philbrook Auditorium	*Classic Films* are shown weekly.
Philbrook Auditorium	A *Summer Lawn Series* includes films, theater and concerts.

The *Museum Shop* carries exhibition catalogs, art books, imported folk art, museum replicas and original craft work by regional artisans.

Changing Exhibitions are regularly featured.

Hours: Monday–Saturday, 10 A.M.–5 P.M.; Sunday, 1 P.M.–5 P.M. *Closed:* Legal holidays.

Admission: Adults, $1.50; college students with I.D. and senior citizens over 65, 75¢. Children high school age and younger, free.

**THOMAS GILCREASE INSTITUTE OF
AMERICAN HISTORY AND ART
1400 North 25 West Ave.
Tulsa, OK 74127
Tel: (918)581-5311**

The institute was founded in 1942, to implement Thomas Gilcrease's desire to preserve man's story in the Western hemisphere. There are collected here approximately half a million works of art, artifacts, history and documents concerned with the Western hemisphere dating from prehistoric to modern times. In 1973, a new system of cataloging was evolved endowing the collection with a coherence and relevance making it still more meaningful.

SAMPLING THE COLLECTION

GEORGE CATLIN
American, 1796–1872

Self-Portrait
1825
Oil on canvas

Catlin's paintings of Indian life serve as important historical representations of the Old West.

JOHN WESLEY JARVIS
British/American, 1780–1840

Black Hawk and His Son,
Whirling Thunder
1833
Oil on canvas

Jarvis taught himself to paint, becoming a successful portraitist and miniaturist. He executed forceful likenesses of celebrated people.

THOMAS EAKINS
American, 1844–1916

Frank Hamilton Cushing
1895
Oil on canvas

After being expelled as a teacher from the Pennsylvania Academy of Fine Arts for posing a nude male model before his class, Eakins painted mostly portraits in radiant tones with great fidelity.

ALBERT BIERSTADT
American, 1830–1902

Sierra Nevada Morning
Oil on canvas

Sketches Bierstadt made on a Western trip were bases for future paintings. His dramatic panoramic landscapes of the American wilderness were immediately popular.

THOMAS MORAN
American, 1837–1926

Grand Canyon
1913
Oil on canvas

Moran, a later Hudson River School painter, like Bierstadt, painted huge landscapes of Western scenery. His earlier sketches were less bombastic and more intimate.

FREDERIC REMINGTON
American, 1861–1909

Coming and Going of the
Pony Express
1900
Oil on canvas

Remington was a rancher, writer and sculptor as well as a painter. His romantic renditions of Indian wars and daily life on the plains are realistically detailed.

CHARLES MARION RUSSELL
American, 1864–1926

Meat's Not Meat Till It's
in the Pan
1915
Oil on canvas

In his youth Russell worked as a cowhand. Known as the "Cowboy Artist," his action-packed canvases of Indians and Western themes are rendered in vivid color.

FACILITIES

Lectures, Gallery Talks and *Films* are offered as special events.

The *Research Library* contains rare documents, manuscripts, maps, photographs and books.

The *Museum Shop* stocks Indian jewelry, prints and reproductions and books.

Hours: Monday–Saturday, 9 A.M.–5 P.M.; Sunday, 1 P.M.–5 P.M. *Closed:* Christmas.

Admission: Free.

WORLD MUSEUM/ART CENTRE
1400 East Skelly Dr.
Tulsa, OK 74105
Tel: (918)743-6233

Founded in 1963, the museum's modern style reflects the shape of the early prairie "schooners" that crossed Oklahoma. The collection, housed in 25 galleries, ranges from prehistoric times to this century and offers examples from over 100 nations. It contains marble, bronze and wood statuary; over 500 oil paintings including 16th to 18th-century Masters; prints, etchings and engravings; photographs of 19th-century Indian chiefs; European and American decorative arts; Papua, New Guinea, aboriginal art; African tribal art; Oriental art; Asian musical instruments; modern metal art; classic cars and buggies and farm tools.

SAMPLING THE COLLECTION

Fine Arts Area, Grand Gallery

PETER PAUL RUBENS
Flemish, 1577–1640

The Nativity
Oil on canvas

Rubens is the most celebrated painter of the northern Baroque. His output was enormous and he employed a horde of assistants who helped him turn out his highly successful work.

Fine Arts Area

CHARLES LE BRUN
French, 1619–1690

Crucifix with Angels
Oil on canvas

Le Brun, court painter to Louis XIV, enhanced the king's public image on canvas and decorated his palaces. A founder and director of the French Academy, he inaugurated the precepts to which it adhered.

Fine Arts Area

GUSTAVE DORE
French, 1833–1883

Vale of Tears
1882
Oil on canvas

Doré is best known for his wood-engraved book illustrations executed with great technical ability. He produced few paintings and those mostly late in life.

Marble Gallery

LOUIS ERNEST BARRIAS
French, 1841–1905

Le Serment de Spartacus
1871
Marble

Barrias was a Classicist who came from a family of artists. His father was a respected miniaturist and his brother painted historical scenes.

FACILITIES

Hours: *Winter:* Daily, 10 A.M.–6 P.M. *Summer:* Daily, 10 A.M.–6 P.M. *Closed:* Christmas.

Admission: Adults, $2.50; students, $1.75; children, $1; children under 6, free.

Imperial Jade Memorial Pagoda. *Courtesy University of Oregon Museum of Art Collection, Eugene*

OREGON

EUGENE

UNIVERSITY OF OREGON MUSEUM OF ART
Eugene, OR 97403
Tel: (503)686-3027

Built in 1932 to house a large Oriental collection which had been given to the university, the museum now owns a collection which has expanded to include not only fine and decorative arts from China, Japan, Korea, Cambodia, and India, but also works from the entire Pacific Basin. Works by contemporary artists of the Pacific Northwest are featured in a permanent exhibition gallery, and the museum is increasingly collecting a broad range of American and European paintings, graphics and crafts. The courtyard and reflecting pool serve to display pieces from the contemporary sculpture holdings and an active changing loan exhibition program complements the permanent installations.

SAMPLING THE COLLECTION

CHINESE	*Imperial Jade Memorial Pagoda*	**2nd Floor**
Ch'ing Dynasty, 1644–1912	ca. 1709	**Gallery,**

This is a nine-storied pagoda constructed of "moss-in-snow" jade with pink **Throne Room** glass doors and metal roof spines and 80 wind bells. Seventy inches high, it is installed on a carved, black wood stand. This structure was commissioned by the Emperor K'ang Hsi on the occasion of the birth of his grandson, the future Emperor Ch'ien Lung.

FACILITIES

The *Showcase Gallery* features works by Oregon artists for sale or rent. Sale prices from $50.

The *Rainbow Gift Shop* sells small antiques, imported objects, jewelry, cards and slides from the museum's collection; fabrics, crafts and toys. A wide variety of prices.

Hours: Tuesday–Sunday, 12 P.M.–5 P.M. *Closed:* Mondays, and during the university's academic breaks.

Admission: Free.

PORTLAND

PORTLAND ART MUSEUM
1219 Southwest Park
Portland, OR 97205
Tel: (530)226-2811

Founded in 1892, the museum is one of the two oldest art museums on the West Coast. Just five blocks south of downtown Portland, the brick and travertine building was designed in 1931 by Pietro Belluschi, also the consultant for the adjoining art school which blends well with the original building. A pedestrian mall embellished by sculpture runs along the north side of the museum. A sculpture court accented by a skylight enhances the entrance area. The permanent collection is composed of a selective view of many of the important art traditions of the world. It includes Northwest Indian art of the early inhabitants of the coast of British Columbia and Alaska, featuring ceremonial and utilitarian objects; Cameroon art of Africa, "a kind of microcosm of the whole world of African art"; pre-Columbian art of the Americas containing ceramics, textiles, works in gold and carved stone from the ancient civilizations of Middle and South America to the Spanish Conquest; Asian art with examples of Chinese bronzes, ceramics, stone sculpture, paintings, furniture and Japanese prints and screens; Classical art with vases from 5th-century Athens and from 4th-century Greek cities of Italy, Roman lamps, bucchero ware, Mediterranean glass vessels and more; English silver by 18th-century Huguenot silversmiths exhibited with furnishings and paintings of the period; art of the Renaissance containing Italian and Northern European paintings and sculpture from the 14th century on; post-Renaissance European art rich in Italian, Flemish, Dutch, German and English Masters; 20th-century art including German Expressionism and American art.

SAMPLING THE COLLECTION

PAINTINGS

North Ayer Gallery
FOLLOWER OF BERNARDO DADDI
Italian, Florentine,
1290–1348

The Aldobrandini Triptych,
Madonna Surrounded by Saints
ca. 1336
Tempera on wood

The central panel represents the Madonna enthroned surrounded by angels and saints. The other wings depict the Annunciation, the Nativity and the Crucifixion. Daddi linked aspects of Giotto's work with Sienese style.

North Ayer Gallery
LUCAS CRANACH, THE ELDER
German, 1472–1553

Madonna and Child with
St. Catherine
Oil on panel

Although influenced by Dürer, Cranach's paintings express a gaiety not found in Dürer's work. The finished character of his paintings was accomplished by a valid, precise technique.

North Ayer Gallery
BERNARDO STROZZI
Italian, 1581–1644

St. Lawrence Giving the
Treasures of the Church to
the Poor
ca. 1635–1640
Oil on canvas

From 1631, Strozzi, a Capuchin friar, resided and worked in Venice to escape his church ties. Here, his animated religious and genre paintings were achieved with a lighter palette.

South Ayer Gallery
FRANCOIS BOUCHER
French, 1703–1770

Portrait of Mme de Pompadour
Oil on canvas

Boucher's Rococo style demonstrates the personal "realism" preferred by 18th-century France to the "grand style" previously admired. His paintings record a frivolous life-style. Favored by Mme. de Pompadour, he painted her several times.

JEAN BAPTISTE GREUZE   *The Drunken Cobbler*   **South**
French, 1725–1805   Oil on canvas   **Ayer**
Greuze's paintings were popular in his lifetime. He painted mainly portraits and **Gallery** moralistic, didactic genre scenes, often accompanied by explanatory letters to the public.

EUGENE DELACROIX   *Christ on the Lake of*   **South**
French, 1798–1863   *Genezareth*   **Ayer**
    1853   **Gallery**
    Oil on canvas
Delacroix was the great romantic painter of the 19th century. Influenced by English handling of color, his freely executed canvases became increasingly rich in color.

PIERRE AUGUSTE RENOIR   *The Seine at Argenteuil*   **South**
French, 1841–1919   1873   **Ayer**
    Oil on canvas   **Gallery**
This canvas was executed at the time Renoir and Monet were painting outdoors together. The broken color style they developed would come to be known as Impressionism.

CHAIM SOUTINE   *Le Petit Patissier*   **Central**
Lithuanian/French, 1894–1943   ca. 1922   **Ayer**
    Oil on canvas   **Gallery**
Soutine was an Expressionist. His morbid, distorted paintings are expressed in violent color and brushwork. His mature work became less tortured.

MARSDEN HARTLEY   *After the Storm*   **Central**
American, 1877–1943   Oil on canvas   **Ayer**
Hartley's early work is associated with German Expressionism. His mature **Gallery** paintings are concerned with the New England landscape, strongly outlined and harshly colored.

ALBERT BIERSTADT   *Mt. Hood*   **Central**
American, 1830–1902   1869   **Ayer**
    Oil on canvas   **Gallery**
Bierstadt was a successful painter throughout his career, committing to canvas monumental romantic landscapes of the American Western wilderness.

JAPANESE   *The Shrine of Itsukushima*   **Asian**
Edo Period, 1615–1868   2nd half of 17th c.   **Gallery**
    Screen, paint on gold ground
Japanese culture flourished during the Edo period when outside influences were excluded. Important paintings were done on screens, sliding doors and wall spaces. Realism sometimes approached scientific precision.

SCULPTURE AND FURNITURE

MEXICAN   *Hierophant*   **pre-Colum-**
Veracruz, Cocuite Culture,   Clay   **bian**
A.D. 600–900   **Gallery**
This priest figure was executed in the Late Classic period, a time in Mexican history when great civilizations were built and the arts flourished.

| pre-Colum-
bian Gallery | MEXICAN
Veracruz, Cocuite Culture,
A.D. 600–900 | *Ritual Ball Player*
Clay |

The sacred ball game was related to human sacrifice. Elaborate paraphernalia was worn by the participants and the losing captain was sacrificed by the victors.

| Northwest
Coast
Indian
Gallery | ALASKAN
Juneau, Tlingit People | *Wolf Hat*
Carved wood, painted black, red,
blue green |

Carved and painted wooden hats are among the Tlingits' finest sculpture. Worn by wealthy men on formal occasions, decorations indicate family or clan affiliations and the importance and affluence of the owner.

| Asian
Gallery | CHINESE
Pre-Han Dynasty, before 206 B.C. | *Standing Horse*
Wood |

Extreme humidity helped to preserve wooden objects. This figure probably survived in a damp tomb.

| Asian
Gallery | CHINESE
Ming Dynasty, 1368–1644 | *Ch'uang (couch)*
Huang-hua-li wood (light
rosewood) |

Ming furniture is elegant and simple without tapered forms or rounded edges. Decoration was restrained and part of the basic design. No nails and little glue were used.

| Central
Ayer
Gallery | CONSTANTIN BRANCUSI
Rumanian/French, 1876–1957 | *Muse*
1918
Bronze on stone base |

Brancusi refined shapes in a reductive style executing highly polished, flawless, conceptual pieces. They are based on few themes and depend heavily on the material for their forms.

FACILITIES

Guided Tours and *Lectures* are offered.

Temporary Exhibitions culled from the museum's collection or *Loan Exhibitions* from other institutions are regular features of the museum's program.

The *Film Study Center* regularly screens a variety of classic and educational films. Call for program.

The *Museum Reference Library* houses art books, periodicals, museum bulletins, exhibition catalogs and color slides. Open Tuesday–Friday, 9 A.M.–5 P.M.; Saturdays, 12 P.M.–3 P.M.

The *Sales and Rental Gallery* contains original works of art. Hours: Tuesday–Friday, 12 P.M.–5 P.M.; Sunday, 2 P.M.–5 P.M.

Hours: Tuesday–Sunday, 12 P.M.–5 P.M.; Friday evening, 5 P.M.–10 P.M.
     Closed: Mondays.

Admission: A contribution is requested. Adults, $1; students, 50¢; senior citizens and children 12 and under are not asked to contribute.

TEXAS

AUSTIN

HUNTINGTON GALLERY, UNIVERSITY ART MUSEUM
University of Texas
23rd and San Jacinto Sts.
Austin, TX 78705
Tel: (512)471-7324

HRC GALLERY, UNIVERSITY ART MUSEUM
Harry Ransom Center
University of Texas
21st and Guadalupe
Austin, TX 78705
Tel: (512)471-7324

The Huntington Gallery is located in the Art Building, which was dedicated in 1963. The collection emphasizes the art of the Americas. It contains Latin American paintings and drawings; etchings; woodcuts and engravings. The HRC Gallery, opened in the Humanities Research Center in 1969, houses the James A. Michener Collection of 20th-century American painting donated by the author and his wife.

SAMPLING THE COLLECTION

HRC GALLERY

ARSHILE GORKY
Armenian/American, 1904–1948

The Dialogue of the Edge (Study for Dark Green Painting)
ca. 1946
Oil on canvas

Michener
Galleries

This painting was executed in Gorky's mature style, two years before his suicide. He combined Surrealist inspiration with Picasso's influence and free painterly brush strokes on canvases that presaged the Abstract Expressionist movement.

PHILIP GUSTON
Canadian/American, 1913–1980

The Alchemist
1960
Oil on canvas

Michener
Galleries

Guston, once a figurative painter, evolved his own brand of lyrical Abstract Expressionism sometimes dubbed Abstract Impressionism. *The Alchemist* forecasts his return to object painting by suggesting a reemergence of form.

HANS HOFMANN
German/American, 1880–1966

Elysium
1960
Oil on canvas

Michener
Galleries

Hans Hofmann, Elysium. *Courtesy James and Mari Michener Collection, University Art Museum, University of Texas at Austin*

Hofmann, both painter and teacher, influenced the course of modern American painting. *Elysium*, a mature work, floats brightly colored, hard-edged rectangles on a setting of diverse hues and tones.

FACILITIES

Hours: Monday–Saturday, 9 A.M.–5 P.M.; Sunday, 1 P.M.–5 P.M. *Closed:* School holidays, but open during summer.

Admission: Free.

CORPUS CHRISTI

ART MUSEUM OF SOUTH TEXAS
1902 North Shoreline Dr.
Corpus Christi, TX 78402
Tel: (512)884-3844

The museum, originally established in 1960, was replaced in 1972 by a sculpturally stunning reinforced concrete contemporary structure designed by Philip Johnson, which is an outstanding attraction. With the exception of bronze-tinted glass openings, affording striking views of the bay, the three-level building is entirely white. On the first floor, the Great Hall, a spacious central area, houses large collections, while adjacent to it, a smaller gallery, with lowered ceiling, offers the intimacy to best display smaller objects. A 60-foot walkway, on the second floor, overlooks the Great Hall and leads to the outdoor sculpture court and the skylighted Upper Gallery. The collections include paintings, sculpture, graphics and photographs of mainly 20th-century American artists.

SAMPLING THE COLLECTION

JENNIFER BARTLETT　　　　　*Untitled*
American, b. 1941　　　　　1976
　　　　　　　　　　　　Ink, colored pencil on graph paper
This piece is a study for a larger work.

JANET FISH　　　　　　　*Blue Grass*
American, b. 1938　　　　　1976
　　　　　　　　　　　　Pastel on paper
Fish is a "photo realist" whose subject matter is always that of empty and half-empty bottles where the light is reflected on and through the bottle.

DONALD JUDD　　　　　　*Untitled*
American, b. 1928　　　　　1977
　　　　　　　　　　　　Pencil on paper
This drawing is of a piece of sculpture in the museum. Judd is a Minimalist whose work lacks association with the outside world. He uses industrial materials in geometric shapes.

MICHAEL TRACY　　　　　*Passage Ritual Drawing*
American, b. 1944　　　　　1976
　　　　　　　　　　　　Oil and acrylic on red Roman
　　　　　　　　　　　　paper
This series of eight pieces is a direct descendant of Abstract Expressionism. Tracy is called a "ritual" artist whose work has developed from ancient cultural forms, like altarpieces of Romanesque churches.

FACILITIES

Lectures are offered to the public.

Films for adults and also for children are screened.

Changing Exhibitions are regularly featured.

The *Library*, a noncirculating research facility, is open Tuesday to Friday, 10 A.M.–5 P.M.

The *Museum Shop* sells books, gifts and handcrafted items.

Hours: Tuesday–Saturday, 10 A.M.–5 P.M.; Sunday, 1 P.M.–5 P.M. *Closed:* Mondays, New Year's, Memorial Day, July 4, Labor Day, Thanksgiving, Christmas.

Admission: Free.

DALLAS

DALLAS MUSEUM OF FINE ARTS
Fair Park
Dallas, TX 75226
Tel: (214)421-4187

Although the collection was founded in 1909, it was not until 1936 that permanent quarters were erected. The original shellstone building was part of the Texas Centennial Exposition. It has been enlarged twice, once in 1964 and again in 1975, and contains 21 galleries, two exhibition lounges and a two-story sculpture court. The collection's primary strength is concentrated in 3,000 pre-Columbian antiquities ranging from 1100 B.C. to A.D. 1500 and includes Olmec objects, Middle American pottery and ceramics and Peruvian gold, silver and textiles. Significant also is the African sculpture collection of more than 300 pieces from the Congo and Central African area dating from the early 1800s to the present. Another area of strength is exhibited in the modern and contemporary collection featuring work by Impressionist, Cubist, Abstract Expressionist, Pop Art, Color Field, Hard Edge and Conceptual artists. Additionally, there is Oceanic, Oriental and Classical art as well as traditional American paintings and Old Masters works.

SAMPLING THE COLLECTION

The permanent collection is regularly rotated; therefore the following works may not always be viewed.

COLOMBIAN
Colima Culture, A.D. 400–700

Diadem: Central Head Engulfed by Crested Crocodile
Gold

Untouched by the complexities of greater Mexican cities, the art of this area was free of gods, death and symbolism; instead it depicted a simple, cheerful daily routine.

MEXICAN
Veracruz (?), A.D. 600–900

Seated Man with Shoulder Tabs
Ceramic

Strong sculptures were executed in a variety of subjects. This man, wearing a necklace, earplugs and other ornaments, sits cross-legged in a typically stylized pose.

MEXICAN
Mixtec Culture, 900–1494

Head of Tlaloc
Ceramic

Mythology and symbolism are prominent in Mixtec art, outstanding for its workmanship. Two large guardian frogs flank the colossal *Head of Tlaloc,* the rain god, one of the most important Mixtec deities.

Seated Man with Shoulder Tabs. *Courtesy Dallas Museum of Fine Arts, Dallas, the Nora and John Wise Collection, Loan*

AFRICAN   *Nimba Headdress*
Sudan, Baga Tribe   Wood
Baga art blended geometric and naturalistic designs. This headdress was used in ceremonial dances.

AFRICAN   *Rhythm Pounder (Déblé)*
Ivory Coast, Northern Region,   Wood, red abrus seeds, cowry
Sikasso District, Senufo Tribe   shells
Senufo sculpture is related to that of the Ivory Coast and of the Sudan, fusing conventionalized forms with naturalistic ones.

CONSTANTIN BRANCUSI   *Beginning of the World*
Rumanian/French, 1876–1957   ca. 1920
                                 Marble, polished metal
Brancusi concentrated on few themes. This piece evolved from the *Sleeping*

Muse, a detached ovoid shape lying on its side that he continued to reduce and simplify into a polished basic egg shape.

HENRI MATISSE   *Ivy in Flower*
French, 1869–1954   1953
                               Collage

In his later work Matisse employed colored cutouts in linear fashion that were considered among his finest achievements.

JACKSON POLLOCK   *Cathedral*
American, 1912–1956   1947
                               Oil on canvas

                               Portrait and a Dream
                               1953
                               Oil on canvas

Although Pollock is most widely known for pouring and dripping paint directly onto unstretched canvas in an overall design, he also painted with brushes.

HENRY MOORE   *Two-Piece Reclining Figure, No. 3*
British, b. 1898   1961
                               Bronze

Primitive cultures and natural forms influence Moore's sculpture. The reclining figure, a recurrent theme, is often executed in two or three pieces, allowing the viewer to walk through them.

DAVID SMITH   *Cubi XVII*
American, 1906–1965   1963
                               Stainless steel

Having worked as a welder in his youth, welded steel became Smith's favorite medium. The simplified sculptures of the *Cubi* series reflect the atmosphere from polished and abraded surfaces.

BARBARA HEPWORTH   .   *Sea Form (Atlantic)*
British, 1903–1975   1964
                               Bronze

                               Contrapuntal Forms (Mycenae)
                               1965
                               Marble

Landscape was the subject matter of many of Hepworth's sculptures, but always in relation to man. She is known for abstract pierced works and fine finishes.

ROBERT MOTHERWELL   *Elegy to the Spanish Republic 108*
American, b. 1915   *(The Barcelona Elegy)*
                               1966
                               Oil on canvas

Motherwell has painted this theme about 150 times. Black oval shapes alternate with upright rectangular ones expressing Motherwell's concern with the Spanish Revolution.

FACILITIES

Gallery Talks are scheduled on Wednesday, 11 A.M.

Lectures are offered by curators or visiting authorities on art issues or exhibitions on Wednesday, 11 A.M.

Temporary Exhibitions culled from the museum's collection or *Loan Exhibitions* from other institutions are regular features of the museum's program.

Concerts by professional musicians are presented two Sundays monthly.

Dance programs are occasionally offered.

The *Museum Shop* carries books, gifts, accessories, handcrafted articles, cards and reproductions beginning at 10¢ for matches with Tom Wesselman's *Mouth #11* from the collection to $500 items.

The *Library,* a noncirculating research facility, houses documentary material emphasizing the permanent collection. A resource room contains slides, files of biographical material on local and international artists and reference slides to other museum collections.

A *Children's Program* is available on weekends during the school term and daily during the summer to teach about art, the museum and the collection through drama, art projects, music and action games.

Films pertaining to current exhibitions are screened on Sunday, 2 P.M. First come, first served. **Auditorium**

The *Gallery Buffet* serves luncheon on Tuesday–Friday, 11:30 A.M.–1:30 P.M. $3 per person. **Lower Level**

Guided Tours on Tuesday, Thursday, Friday, 11 A.M., Wednesday, 1 P.M., Sunday, 2 P.M., at 3 P.M. when films are shown. **Meet at Museum Shop Area**

Hours: Tuesday–Saturday, 10 A.M.–5 P.M.; Sunday, holidays, 1 P.M.–5 P.M.
            Closed: Mondays, Christmas.

Admission: Free.

MEADOWS MUSEUM
SOUTHERN METHODIST UNIVERSITY
Owen Arts Center
Dallas, TX 75275
Tel: (214)692-2516

The museum was founded in 1965 and is located in the Owen Arts Center, a teaching facility for all the arts. Since top quality art is rare and costly today the donor, Algur Meadows, and the university agreed to the emphasis on one area of interest, Spanish art. They chose only the finest examples from the Renaissance to the 20th century. The 104 paintings and drawings plus 242 etchings preserve and permit the study of Spanish art in the Southwestern United States.

SAMPLING THE COLLECTION

Because the galleries are rearranged from time to time, the following locations may not apply.

JUSEPE RIBERA   *St. Paul the Hermit*   **1st Floor,**
Spanish, 1591–1652   1620–1625   **West Gallery**
                      Oil on canvas
Several copies of this painting exist. The brushwork, closely related to Ribera's

well-documented early painting, *St. Jerome,* in the church in Osuna, Spain, leads to the belief that this is the original of many related versions.

Portrait of a Knight of Santiago
1630s
Oil on canvas

Few portraits by Ribera are known. This powerful state portrait is the only one of its type. With the impasto relief and subtle glazes still intact, it shows his unique brushwork. Portraits with spectacles are unusual from this period.

1st Floor,   ANTONIO PEREDA   *St. Joseph and the Christ Child*
West Gallery Spanish, 1608–1678   1655
                                                 Oil on canvas

This overlife-size mature work is a companion piece to *St. Anthony of Padua and the Christ Child* (Hispanic Society of America, New York). The flesh tones of the sensitively rendered Child are highlighted by warm light, the brushwork, free and painterly.

1st Floor,   DIEGO RODRIGUEZ DE SILVA Y
West Gallery VELAZQUEZ   *Portrait of King Philip IV*
                 Spanish, 1599–1660   1623–1624
                                                 Oil on canvas

Velázquez was painter and friend to Philip. This portrait of the 19-year-old king is the earliest by Velázquez in existence. Rejecting customary court portraiture, he communicates the monarch's exalted position through a candid depiction in ordinary clothing.

Sibyl with "Tabula Rasa"
1644–1648
Oil on canvas

Influenced by the paintings of Titian at the court, Velázquez's early naturalistic style evolved into an easier, more extemporaneous one. He is considered the greatest of all Spanish painters.

Portrait of Queen Mariana
ca. 1656
Oil on canvas

This late portrait was painted about the same time as *Las Meninas*. The queen's image and that reflected in the mirror in *Las Meninas* are the same. Velázquez designed the hair styles and costumes for the court ladies.

1st Floor,   BARTOLOME ESTEBAN MURILLO   *The Immaculate Conception*
Central   Spanish, 1617–1682   1655–1660
Gallery   Oil on canvas

Murillo frequently painted this theme. In the Book of Revelation, St. John envisions the Virgin standing upon the moon, her back to the sun crowned with a corona of twelve stars. This is its most common representation.

Jacob Laying the Peeled Rods Before the Flocks of Laban
1665–1670
Oil on canvas

This is one of the remaining four of a series of five monumental Baroque paintings Murillo executed on the life of Jacob. Within the dreamy landscape, the brushwork creates a perception of movement and time.

Diego Rodríguez de Silva y Velázquez, Portrait of Queen Mariana. *Courtesy Meadows Museum, Southern Methodist University, Dallas*

FRANCISCO GOYA Y LUCIENTES
Spanish, 1746–1828

The Madhouse at Saragossa
1793–1794
Oil on canvas

**2nd Floor,
West Gallery**

In 1792 Goya became deaf. While convalescing he created a theme original in art, paintings executed from observation filled with fantasy and invention. Here strong light does not brighten but rather casts dark shadows on the psychotic inmates.

Los Caprichos

Los Desastres de la Guerra

La Tauromaquia

Los Proverbios
First edition prints

All prints are rotated from time to time. Bitter satire on social institutions and mores lay beneath Goya's seemingly humorous etchings. They were executed in a ruthless, realistic manner.

PABLO PICASSO
Spanish, 1881–1973

Sonnets of Gongora
On Japanese paper

**2nd Floor,
West Gallery**

Picasso's prints were some of the most esthetic and skillful of all time.

2nd Floor,
East Gallery

Still Life in a Landscape
1915
Oil on canvas

This painting in Synthetic Cubist style, with interacting planes and shapes demonstrating spatial relationships, is similar to Picasso's painted sculptures. It provides a link between this period and the Surrealist one to follow.

FACILITIES

Gallery Talks may be arranged in English or Spanish for groups.

A *Catalog* of the collection is available, $7.50.

Hours: Monday–Saturday, 10 A.M.–5 P.M.; Sunday, 1 P.M.–5 P.M. *Closed:*
         Christmas, New Year's.

Admission: Free.

EL PASO

EL PASO MUSEUM OF ART
1211 Montana Ave.
El Paso, TX 79902
Tel: (915)543-3800

The museum is housed in the 1910 mansion of a former Texas senator. From 1947 until 1960 it was known as the International Museum and displayed items of historical interest. With the addition of two new wings in 1960 it was renamed the El Paso Museum of Art. A Kress collection of Early Renaissance, High Renaissance and Baroque-Rococo works are on permanent exhibition in the west wing. The two east wing galleries are devoted to changing exhibitions. A special case in the reception room, once the formal living room and ballroom, features the Treasure of the Month. The Heritage Gallery displays decorative arts from the 18th through the early 20th centuries. Two other associate museums exist in the city system. The *Cavalry Museum* exhibits major dioramas and displays dealing with borderland history and the "Man on Horseback" concept. The *Wilderness Park Museum* of El Paso is a science museum using prehistory area Indians and cultures as theme material. There are major dioramas on Cave Valley Mexico, the Hueco tanks site, Paleo Indian hunting and gathering and the Pueblo period.

SAMPLING THE COLLECTION

The following paintings may not always be on view; they are rotated for exhibition.

CANALETTO (GIOVANNI ANTONIO
CANAL)
Italian, Venetian, 1697–1768

View of the Molo
ca. 1730s
Oil on canvas

Canaletto was a view painter who worked in England as well as in Italy. His paintings of this period are clearer and done in cooler tones than his earlier work.

FREDERIC REMINGTON
American, 1861–1909

Sign of Friendship
1904
Oil on canvas

Remington recorded Western life in carefully detailed academic paintings and sculpture.

GEORGE INNESS
American, 1825–1894

Landscape
1842
Oil on canvas

This canvas was finished soon after Inness began to paint, while he was still influenced by the artists of the Hudson River School.

FACILITIES

Changing Exhibitions of the work of a variety of artists are regular museum features.

The *Reference Library* is open to interested persons upon request during staff hours. It contains books, periodicals, films and related materials.

The *Museum Shop* sells prints, reproductions, Alva replicas and pottery and jewelry created by local craftsmen.

A *Lecture, Demonstration, Recital* or *Film* on art-related topics is presented to the public one Sunday each month. **Auditorium, Lower Level**

Hours: Tuesday–Saturday, 10 A.M.–5 P.M.; Sunday, 1 P.M.–5 P.M. *Closed:* Mondays, national holidays.

Admission: Free.

FORT WORTH

AMON CARTER MUSEUM OF WESTERN ART
3501 Camp Bowie
Fort Worth, TX 76107
Tel: (817)738-1933

The museum, designed by Philip Johnson, was opened in 1961 and stands as an architectural landmark above Fort Worth. Built of Texas shellstone with an interior of bronze and teak, its five segmental arches form an open porch overlooking terrace areas. The museum, concerned with American culture from East to West with its native and imported traditions, places special emphasis on the West. American landscapes, both urban and rural, are the focal point of the permanent collection; the interpreters range from Worthington Whittredge to Ben Shahn. Still-life painting from the 19th century is well represented as are America's premier Western artists.

SAMPLING THE COLLECTION

These pictures may not always be on view; the museum exhibits the permanent collection on a rotating basis.

Exterior view. Courtesy Amon Carter Museum, Fort Worth

MARTIN JOHNSON HEADE   *Thunderstorm over*
American, 1819–1904   *Narragansett Bay*
1868
Oil on canvas

Heade painted atmospheric landscapes with meticulous care. This canvas is acknowledged by most critics to be his best.

WILLIAM MICHAEL HARNETT   *Attention Company!*
Irish/American, 1848–1892   1878
Oil on canvas

Ease
1887
Oil on canvas

Harnett was a trompe-l'oeil painter of still life who chose simple subjects and reproduced them with great accuracy. His realistic renditions of printed matter often looked pasted, anticipating the advent of collage.

FREDERIC REMINGTON   *A Dash for the Timber*
American, 1861–1909   1889
Oil on canvas

The Fall of the Cowboy
1895
Oil on canvas

The Old Stagecoach of the Plains
1901
Oil on canvas

A Dash for the Timber is Remington's masterpiece. Its size, concentrated action, drama, detail and realism combine to achieve a compelling portrayal of Western life. The latter examples are nocturnals, a style practiced by Remington in later years.

FACILITIES

Changing Exhibitions from the permanent collection as well as *Special Exhibitions* concerned with Western events, people and places are featured, as are *Major Exhibitions* by individual painters, sculptors and photographers.

The *Theater Program* features *Lectures, Film Series, Meetings, Symposia, Music Festivals* and *Special Events* all focusing on the overall theme of the museum.

The *Reference Library* may be visited by appointment and specializes in materials of North American art, history and anthropology. It also houses a microfilm collection of 19th-century newspapers and a historic and contemporary photographic collection.

The *Bookstore* sells museum publications and books on a variety of topics in American art and history. Of popular interest are museum posters, prints on paper and canvas, slides, postcards and a Charles Russell brass belt buckle.

Hours: Tuesday–Saturday, 10 A.M.–5 P.M.; Sunday, 1 P.M.–5:30 P.M. *Closed:* Mondays, holidays.

Admission: Free.

FORT WORTH ART MUSEUM
1309 Montgomery St.
Fort Worth, Texas 76107
Tel: (817)738-9215

From its founding in 1901 by a small group of interested patrons, the Fort Worth Art Museum has steadily evolved into a distinguished museum of 20th-century art. Its original collection of late 19th-century paintings housed in the former public library has been greatly expanded to approximately 3,000 works, many of them outstanding examples of contemporary art. A growing collection has led to two expansions of the original building: Fort Worth's first art museum, built by Herbert Bayer in 1954. The latest renovation in 1974 more than doubled the gallery spaces, allowing for more extensive exhibitions and an ever-growing permanent collection.

SAMPLING THE COLLECTION

All work in the permanent collection may not always be on view.

THOMAS EAKINS   *The Swimming Hole*
American, 1844–1916   1883
                                 Oil

Among the major figures in American realist painting of the late 19th century, Thomas Eakins was probably the strongest figure painter. *The Swimming Hole* demonstrates Eakins's ability to incorporate a thorough understanding of human anatomy in a painting that depicts an everyday scene of an afternoon swim in the pond.

PABLO PICASSO   *Femme Couchée Lisant*
Spanish, 1881–1973   1960
                                        Oil

Throughout his long and immensely prolific life Picasso consistently explored new ways of depicting the human form. This painting of a reclining woman reading a book is an excellent example of Picasso's characteristic multipoint perspective in the way that he shows the figure simultaneously from front and side.

ROBERT RAUSCHENBERG   *Whistle Stop*
American, b. 1925   1977
                                        Wooden doors, fabric, photo
                                        collage, graphite drawing, acrylic
                                        wash

Rauschenberg has been in the forefront of the avant-garde since the early 1960s. His work combines everyday objects with the traditional materials of painting and printmaking to make what are essentially large scale collages. The theme of *Whistle Stop* is the railroad, and the piece is dedicated to the artist's father who was a trainman.

FACILITIES

Tours are available for groups of over 12 people. Call at least one week in advance (817)738-6811.

Changing Exhibitions are regularly featured.

Restoration of prints and drawings can be arranged at the museum. Contact Conservator Jacqueline Gilliam (817)738-9215.

The *Library*, a noncirculating reference facility, is open Monday, Wednesday, Friday, 10 A.M.–1 P.M.

Entrance   The *Museum Shop* sells posters, postcards, calendars, art objects, exhibition
Gallery   catalogs, and books on art, film, photography and the performing arts.

Hours: Wednesday–Saturday, 10 A.M.–5 P.M.; Tuesday, 10 A.M.–9 P.M.; Sunday, 1 P.M.–5 P.M. *Closed:* Mondays, most holidays.

Admission: Free.

KIMBELL ART MUSEUM
1101 Will Rogers Rd. W.
Fort Worth, TX 76107
Tel: (817)332-8451

The museum stands in a tree-filled plaza with two open cycloidal vaults facing reflecting pools. Slits admitting natural light run the length of the vaults of post-tensioned concrete which comprise the building. Opened to the public in 1972, the innovative structure was one of the last to be designed by Louis I. Kahn before his death. The collection contains masterpieces from prehistoric times to Picasso.

SAMPLING THE COLLECTION

South   DUCCIO DI BUONINSEGNA   *The Raising of Lazarus*
Galleries Italian, Sienese, fl. 1255–1319   1308–1311
                                                 Oil on canvas

Exterior view. Courtesy Kimbell Art Museum, Fort Worth

This panel is from the great Maestà altarpiece of the Cathedral of Siena. The altarpiece is the only extant work indisputably by Duccio. An outstanding narrative painter, he provided a link between the Byzantine and Gothic styles.

PETER PAUL RUBENS Flemish, 1577–1640	*The Duke of Buckingham* 1625 Oil on canvas	**South** **Galleries**

Rubens was the greatest painter of the northern Baroque. This equestrian portrait was considered lost for 300 years. It is a study for a larger work later destroyed by fire.

EL GRECO (DOMENICOS THEOTOCOPOULOS) Greek, ca. 1541–1614	*Giacomo Bosio* 1600–1610 Oil on canvas	**South** **Galleries**

El Greco's paintings are characterized by their attenuated figures, eerie coloring and overall mysticism.

REMBRANDT HARMENSZ VAN RIJN Dutch, 1606–1669	*Portrait of a Young Jew* 1663 Oil on canvas	**South** **Galleries**

Living in the Jewish Quarter at this time, Rembrandt painted many of its inhabitants. His portraits were executed with keen psychological insight and, as his style matured, he simplified his palette, painting in light and shadow.

ENGLISH	*The Barnabas Altarpiece* 1250–1260 Oil on wood panel	**South** **Galleries**

The Barnabas Altarpiece is the oldest surviving English painting on wood.

FACILITIES

Guided Tours, Lectures, Gallery Talks, Films and *Concerts* are all available. Call for further information.

The *Bookstore* sells postcards, posters, exhibition catalogs, and a variety of books on art history relating to the Kimbell collection. *Catalog of the Kimbell Collection,* $25. *Light is the Theme,* $5.

North End   A *Snack Bar* serves light lunches during regular museum hours.

Hours: Daily, 10 A.M.–5 P.M.; Sunday, 1 P.M.–5 P.M. *Closed:* Mondays, New Year's, July 4, Thanksgiving, Christmas.

Admission: Free.

GALVESTON

ROSENBERG LIBRARY
2310 Sealy Ave.
Galveston, TX 77550
Tel: (713)763-8854

The library, which was founded in 1900, shares its quarters with three galleries displaying art from the 18th to 20th centuries. An addition, the Moody Memorial Wing, was erected in 1971. The art collection is housed mainly in the third floor Harris Gallery.

SAMPLING THE COLLECTION

WORTHINGTON WHITTREDGE   *Along the Platte River,*
American, 1820–1910   *Colorado*
                               Oil
Whittredge's early paintings are associated with the Hudson River School of landscape artists. He traveled to the West in 1865 and thereafter concentrated on Western and Indian landscapes.

THOMAS LAWRENCE   *Hamlet*
British, 1769–1830   Oil
Lawrence's attractive style made his portraits extremely popular. He painted successful likenesses of celebrated figures of the day and became painter to the king.

3rd Floor   *THE LYKES GALLERY*

This gallery traces Galveston's maritime history and includes several fine ship models, paintings and artifacts.

FACILITIES

Lectures, Gallery Talks, Films for adults and children, *Concerts* and *Dance Recitals* are scheduled. Call for program information.

Changing Interpretive Exhibits are regularly featured.

The *Library,* in addition to books, documents and manuscripts contains collections relating to the history of Texas and the Southwest.

Hours: Monday–Thursday, 9 A.M.–9 P.M.; Friday, Saturday, 9 A.M.–6 P.M.;
    Closed: Sundays, national holidays, San Jacinto Day (April 21).

Admission: Free.

HOUSTON

BAYOU BEND COLLECTION OF
THE MUSEUM OF FINE ARTS, HOUSTON
1 Westcott St.
Houston, Texas 77019
Tel: (713)529-8773

Bayou Bend, comprising 24 rooms and settings, is situated at the end of the Buffalo Bayou. The former home and extensive gardens of Ima Hogg and her brothers, children of the late Texas governor, was erected in 1928. Gifted to the Museum of Fine Arts, Houston, it was opened to the public in 1966. The collection contains American decorative art and fine arts spanning 200 years from the 17th-century pilgrim era to that of the mid-19th-century early Victorian. The collection is particularly outstanding in American furniture, paintings, silver and ceramics.

Drawing Room. *Courtesy Bayou Bend Collection of the Museum of Fine Arts, Houston*

SAMPLING THE COLLECTION

JEREMIAH DUMMER
American, Boston,
Massachusetts, 1645–1718

Tankard
1690–1700
Silver

Beer, ale and hard cider, popular dinner drinks in early America, warranted large drinking vessels. A tankard was an outsized lidded mug. Dummer, born in America, was the first native-trained silversmith.

CHARLES WILLSON PEALE
American, 1741–1827

*Self-Portrait with Wife
(Rachel) and Daughter
(Angelica Kauffman)*
ca. 1788
Oil on canvas

Peale, the most prominent member in a family of painters, executed several insightful self-portraits as well as conversation pieces of the Peale family. Here, we see a combined effort.

MURPHY ROOM

This room, furnished in William and Mary style, is the earliest period, 1650–1725, represented at Bayou Bend. The painted floor, imitating marble, is a decorative scheme used at that time.

FACILITIES

The *Sales Desk* carries books and postcards.

Guided Tours of approximately two hours include a rest period. Groups of four are escorted by trained guides. Women are requested not to wear high-heeled shoes as they easily damage floors and carpets. Slippers are provided for those who do not comply. Guests are asked to register 15 minutes prior to the scheduled tour.

Reservations are required for admission and may be made by writing to the Tour Secretary, P.O. Box 13157, Houston, TX 77019, or by telephoning (713)-529-8773. Specify alternate dates. A $1 deposit is necessary to hold reservations. It is refundable on arrival or on request for cancellation received 48 hours or more in advance. No one under 16 is admitted.

Family Tours of the first floor are offered on the second Sunday of each month (except March and August), from 1 P.M. to 5 P.M. No reservations are necessary. Children are welcome.

Hours: *Mornings:* Tuesday–Saturday, *2-hour tours begin every 15 minutes,* 10 A.M.–11:15 A.M.; *Afternoons:* Tuesday–Friday, *2-hour tours begin every 15 minutes,* 1:15 P.M.–2:30 P.M.. *Closed:* Weekends, July 4, August, Labor Day, Thanksgiving, Christmas, New Year's.

Admission: Free. Contributions are welcomed.

MUSEUM OF FINE ARTS, HOUSTON
**1001 Bissonnet St.
Houston, TX 77005
Tel: (713)526-1361**

The museum was founded in 1900 as a teaching aid to the city's public schools. It has been housed in its present quarters since 1924. An addition to the classical-style building was designed by Mies van der Rohe and opened in

January 1974. Predominantly glass and steel, it completes a building program that provides a repository for its encyclopedic collection spanning 5,000 years of human creativity from prehistoric times to the present. The collection contains American and European classic and contemporary paintings, graphics, and sculpture, including a collection of 50 paintings that represents almost every major artist of the late 19th and early 20th centuries; American and European decorative arts; Oriental art; pre-Columbian, African and Oceanic artifacts; Western Americana; photography and antiquities.

SAMPLING THE COLLECTION

THE TARGET COLLECTION OF PHOTOGRAPHS

This collection contains photographs spanning the early years of this century to the present.

ROMAN Late Severan Period, ca. 22–230	*Sarcophagus Front: The* *Return of the Body of* *Meleager to Kalydon* Marble	**Lovett** **Gallery**

Early sarcophagi lined in active slate-alum stone, consumed an enclosed body within 40 days. The charioteer on the left of this burial piece, worked in high relief, is probably the deceased.

AFRICAN Mali, Bandiagara Region, Dogon Tribe	*Ark* Wood	**Lower** **Brown** **Galleries**

The ark, a large dark vessel, probably contained water, which was considered a life-symbol force. Water spirits and a horse's head, both primary images in Dogon mythology, adorn the ark.

ROGIER VAN DER WEYDEN Flemish, 1399–1464	*Virgin and Child* Oil on panel	**Upper Jones** **Gallery,** **Straus** **Collection**

In his later panel paintings, Rogier returned to devotional images expressed especially in bust-length depictions of Christ and the Virgin and Child. He created an emotional iconography adopted by later Flemish painters.

JEAN-HONORE FRAGONARD French, 1732–1806	Scene from Ariosto's *Orlando* *Furioso: Rodomonte and* *Madricardo State Their Case* *Before Agramante* Pen and brown and gray wash over chalk	**Blaffer** **Corridor**

This scene is from a series Fragonard drew for Ariosto's medieval romance, *Orlando Furioso.* He is best known for his renditions of the joyful life-style practiced by the French aristocracy.

ANDRE DERAIN French, 1880–1954	*The Turning Road* 1906 Oil on canvas	**Corridor** **Adjacent to** **Lower Jones** **Gallery**

Derain made his greatest contribution to art history in this, his Fauve period. Agitated slashing brushwork of pure color that he called "sticks of dynamite" emit light from his canvases.

Beck **Collection** **Gallery**	GEORGE BELLOWS American, 1882–1925	*Lady with Red Hair* ca. 1920 Oil on canvas

Although Bellows is known for his prizefighting scenes, his early landscapes and mature portraits are outstanding. In the latter, he uses artful variations of color to penetrate his subject's character.

Mullins **Gallery**	GEORGIA O'KEEFFE American, b. 1887	*Grey Line with Black, Blue* *and Yellow* ca. 1923 Oil on canvas

O'Keeffe's own brand of Precisionism is seen in this nonexpressive work painted before she began her semiabstract floral renditions. Smoothly graded vivid colors and amorphic shapes suggest things in nature.

FACILITIES

Three types of *Tours* are offered by Gallery Guides: *Highlights of the Collection* (Tuesday–Saturday at 1 P.M.; *Temporary Exhibitions* and *Gallery of the Week* (all tours at 1 P.M.; tours vary each day).

Ground Floor *Lectures* on art or related topics by noted authorities are offered.

Temporary Exhibitions culled from the museum's collection or *Loan Exhibitions* from other institutions are regular features of the museum's program.

The *Masterson Junior Gallery* provides a series of changing exhibitions of interest to young people that are designed for spontaneous and individual creativity.

Brown *Films* for adults and children of a classic or educational nature are regularly
Auditorium screened. Call for program information.

Brown *Concerts* of classical or jazz music are presented several times monthly.
Auditorium

Brown The *Library* contains books on art history and exhibition catalogs. Closed stack,
Pavilion, noncirculating. Open to the public.
Ground Level

Brown The *Restaurant,* which opens onto a landscaped courtyard, serves hot meals,
Pavilion sandwiches, salads, snacks, desserts and beverages, including beer and wine.

Brown The *Museum Shop* carries items from inexpensive postcards to prints in the
Pavilion $100 range. These, plus replica jewelry and exhibition catalogs, are the most popular purchases.

Hours: Tuesday–Saturday, 10 A.M.–5 P.M.; Sunday, 12 P.M.–6 P.M.. *Closed:* Mondays, New Year's, July 4, Thanksgiving, Christmas.

Admission: Free.

MARSHALL

HARRISON COUNTY HISTORICAL MUSEUM
Old Courthouse
Peter Whetstone Square
Marshall, TX 75670
Tel: (214)938-2680

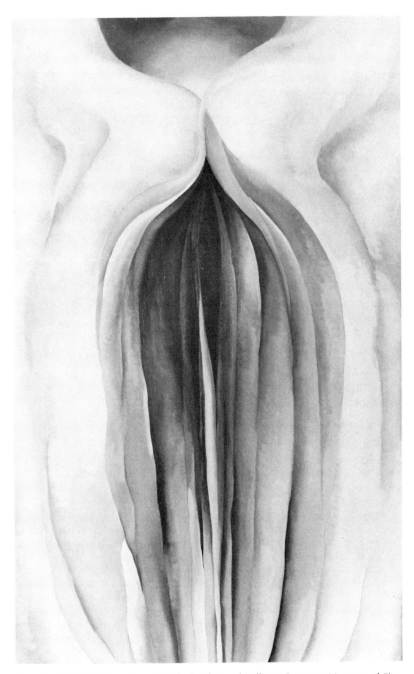

Georgia O'Keeffe, Grey Line with Black, Blue and Yellow. *Courtesy Museum of Fine Arts, Houston. Museum Purchase, Agnes Cullen Arnold Endowment Fund*

The museum, founded in 1965 in a 1901 courthouse, contains ceramics, portraits, timepieces, jewelry, silverware, porcelain, glass, 19th- and early 20th-century musical and audio instruments, needlecraft, transportation, communication and industrial exhibits, mementoes of fraternal lodges, religious, military and political mementoes, celebrity exhibitions and toys.

SAMPLING THE COLLECTION

1st Floor, **Reception** **Office**	TCHEFUNCTE INDIAN	*Pottery* 400 B.C.

Tchefuncte pottery is most usually found in a flowerpot shape with a flat bottom or four short legs and is either buff or gray colored.

1st Floor, **Reception** **Office**	CADDO INDIAN	*Pottery* A.D. 700–1830

Made through the 18th century, but considered pre-Columbian because the designs remained virtually the same, Caddo pottery was hand built. It was plain or brush-roughened, incised, engraved, painted or unpainted.

FACILITIES

A *Sales Desk* carries historical publications.

Hours: Sunday–Friday, 1:30 P.M.–5 P.M. *Closed:* Saturdays, New Year's, Memorial Day, July 4, Labor Day, Thanksgiving, week of December 25.

Admission: Adults, $1; students, 50¢.

ORANGE

STARK MUSEUM OF ART
712 Green Ave.
Orange, TX 77630
Tel: (713)883-6661

In 1978, a contemporary museum building was opened to house one family's collection. It consists chiefly of 19th-and 20th-century American Western paintings and sculpture, with examples from the 1820s to 1970, and a good representation of the original Taos artists. The American Indian collection comprises objects crafted by Great Plains and Southwestern tribes and includes Plains' clothing, body ornaments and beadwork; examples from Western basket-producing cultures; Pueblo pottery; Zuñi and Hopi kachina dolls and Navajo rugs and blankets. There is a complete series of Dorothy Doughty's lifelike porcelain birds and a group of 52 bowls by Steuben Glass entitled, "The United States in Crystal," in which each state is represented by a finely etched scene unique to its history.

SAMPLING THE COLLECTION

Lobby	AMERICAN North Dakota Plains Chippewa Indian	*Pad Saddle* ca. 1890 Beadwork

William Herbert Dunton, McMullin, Guide. *Courtesy Stark Museum of Art, Orange*

Saddles of contoured beadwork originated with the woodland tribes but were later made and used by northern Plains tribes who continued the floral patterns characteristic of woodland beadwork.

ALFRED JACOB MILLER   *Lassoing Wild Horses*   **Gallery 2**
American, 1810–1874   Oil on canvas
Hired in 1837 to record the adventures of a private expedition by a Scottish nobleman through the West, Miller presents a romantic, sometimes anecdotal view of the frontier.

WILLIAM HERBERT DUNTON   *McMullin, Guide*   **Gallery 5**
American, 1878–1936   Oil on canvas

Dunton, an early member of the Taos Society of Artists, was primarily interested in depicting the vanishing Western frontier life. He idealized this cowboy on a perfectly groomed white horse in an ordered forest.

FACILITIES

Changing Exhibitions are regularly featured.

The *Museum Shop* carries books, postcards and posters. There are also catalogs on the *Western Collection,* 1978 ($10); the *Steuben Glass Collection* ($2.50) and the *American and British Birds of Dorothy Doughty* ($2.50).

Hours: Wednesday–Saturday, 10 A.M.–5 P.M.; Sunday, 1 P.M.–5 P.M.. *Closed:* Mondays, Tuesdays, New Year's, Easter, July 4, Thanksgiving, Christmas.

Admission: Free.

SAN ANTONIO

McNAY ART INSTITUTE
6000 North Braunfels
San Antonio, TX 78209
Tel: (512)824-5368

The institute is situated in the hills of San Antonio, on 25 acres, some cultivated and some in native state, which surround the Mediterranean-style mansion built around a large flowering patio. Terraces, balconies and loggias overlook the gardens. The home of Marion Koogler McNay was constructed in 1927. In 1950, her residence and collections were bequeathed to create a museum of modern art. The institute's permanent collection houses the McNay collection, primarily devoted to art of the 19th and 20th centuries with emphasis on the Expressionist tradition; Gothic and medieval art; New Mexican arts and crafts; graphic arts and American painting and sculpture. The Sculpture Pavilion, opened in 1970, along with the Koehler Fountain, 1975, provide a lovely setting for the expanding sculpture collection.

SAMPLING THE COLLECTION

Brown Gallery
BEN NICHOLSON
British, b. 1894
Jan 3–52
1952
Oil on canvas

Nicholson's characteristic works are shallow painted reliefs with simple geometric designs, or partially abstract paintings based on Cubism. Lines almost devoid of meaning sometimes run rampant over the paintings.

Brown Gallery
ARISTIDE MAILLOL
French, 1861–1944
La Nymphe
1930
Bronze

Maillol preferred to model large powerful, but passive, women. He admired the sculpture of ancient Greece and his figures were modeled with the same classical simplicity.

AMADEO MODIGLIANI Italian, 1884–1920	*Girl with Blue Eyes* Oil on canvas	**Gallery 2**

Modigliani's style was unique although he was affected by a variety of influences: Cubism, Fauvism, Expressionism, African sculpture and Botticelli. His faces and figures are marked by their elongated forms, a fine sense of color and superior draftsmanship.

PAUL GAUGUIN French, 1848–1903	*Portrait of the Artist with* *the Idol* ca. 1893 Oil on canvas	**Gallery 2**

During his later years, Gaugin rejected Western civilization to live in the South Seas among primitive people, the subjects of his intensely colored paintings of simplified forms. These nonnaturalistic paintings had a major impact on 20th-century art.

PAUL CEZANNE French, 1839–1906	*Portrait of Henri Gasquet* Oil on canvas	**Gallery 2**

Cézanne believed that the cone, the sphere and the cylinder are to be seen in nature. Using these forms, he modeled from nature with color, thus laying the foundation for Cubism and modern art.

GEORGIA O'KEEFFE American, b. 1887	*From the Plains I* Oil on canvas	**Lang** **Gallery**

O'Keeffe works in an abstracted Precisionist style. Much of her life has been spent in the Southwest where she executes large close-up paintings of natural subjects.

PABLO PICASSO Spanish, 1881–1973	*Portrait of Sylvette* 1954 Oil on canvas	**Lang** **Gallery**

Picasso's work exerted the greatest influence on modern art, undergoing many stylistic changes. Until World War II he was in the vanguard of European art, afterward frequently turning his talents toward ceramics, sculpture and graphic art.

FACILITIES

Guided Tours may be arranged with advance notice.

Public Gallery Talks and *Concerts* are scheduled at intervals.

Changing Exhibitions are regularly featured.

The *Sales Desk* carries postcards of reproductions in the collection (10¢ or 15¢ for color) and catalogs of past exhibitions, 50¢–$10.

Hours: Tuesday–Saturday, 9 A.M.–5 P.M.; Sunday, 2 P.M.–5 P.M.. *Closed:* Mondays, New Year's Day, July 4, Thanksgiving, Christmas.

Admission: Free, but contributions are gratefully accepted.

WICHITA FALLS

WICHITA FALLS MUSEUM AND ART CENTER
2 Eureka Circle
Wichita Falls, TX 76308
Tel: (817)692-0923

The museum, founded in 1965, is located in a parklike setting near a lovely duck pond. Because it is a suburban museum with limited funds it does not attempt to purchase art in competition with heavily endowed institutions but has focused on fine but less costly art. The emphasis is on a historical survey of American art through a collection of graphics or prints. A grant several years ago from the National Endowment for the Arts specified the purchase of works of living American artists and so the collection has special strength in this area.

SAMPLING THE COLLECTION

ALBERT BIERSTADT
American, 1830–1902

Indian Encampment in the Rockies
1875
Chromolithograph

Bierstadt was a success throughout his career. He painted romantic landscapes of the American West. His later work more often portrays Indians and wild animals.

MARY CASSATT
American, 1845–1926

Baby Held Before an Open Window
1910
Drypoint (etching) edition of 5 or less

Cassatt worked with and helped to promote the Impressionists. Her paintings of mothers and children were sensitive and technically able. Her etchings and her color prints, strongly influenced by Japanese woodcuts, are considered her most original work.

CLAES OLDENBURG
American, b. 1929

Letter Q as Beach House with Sailboat
1972
Lithograph 8/100

Oldenburg is best known for his large soft sculptures of malleable materials depicting ordinary objects, electric fans, hamburgers, typewriters, etc. He was one of the originators of Pop Art.

FACILITIES

Guided Tours are available for all ages.

Changing Exhibitions are regularly featured.

Saturday at the Museum offers children the opportunity to spend the day engaged in a variety of activities: a day may be spent on Indian lore and camping or perhaps in celebration of spring's arrival. Cost, $5.

Sunday Fun Day are hour-long film programs for the whole family scheduled every second and fourth Sunday of the month at 1:30 P.M. Free.

Planetarium Shows are held Sunday, 3 P.M. Adults, 80¢; children, 40¢.

The *Library* is available for use on the premises.

The *Sales Desk* carries postcards, candles, puzzles, posters and jewelry.

Hours: Monday–Friday, 9 A.M.–5 P.M.; Saturday, 9 A.M.–4:30 P.M.; Sunday, 1 P.M.–5 P.M. *Closed:* Holidays.

Admission: Free.

UTAH

UTAH MUSEUM OF FINE ARTS
University of Utah
104 AAC
Salt Lake City, UT 84112
Tel: (801)581-7332

The museum, the only public general art museum in Utah, was founded in 1951 on the campus of the University of Utah. It moved into a new building in 1970. In 1975 two new galleries were added to the building situated in the art and architecture complex, making room for the expanding collection that represents the principal artistic styles and periods from prehistory to the present. The collection emphasizes 19th-century American and French landscape painting, 18th-century French decorative arts, 17th–18th century English furniture and pictures, Egyptian antiquities, Buddhist objects, Ch'ing Dynasty porcelains, Navajo weavings and contemporary graphics.

SAMPLING THE COLLECTION

Selections from the permanent collection are regularly rotated so that the following works may not always be on view.

Gallery 4 AMBROSIUS BENSON   *Elegant Couples Dancing*
           Flemish, ca. 1495–1550   *in a Landscape*
                                     ca. 1545
                                     Oil on panel
Although Benson worked and was well known in Bruges, he catered largely to foreigners. The manner in which he graded tones from light to dark helped in attributing certain paintings to him.

Gallery 4 CHARLES LE BRUN   *The Family of Darius Before*
           French, 1619–1690   *Alexander*
                                     ca. 1661
                                     Tapestry
Le Brun, painter to Louis XIV, decorated his palaces and directed the royal tapestry factory. French academism was based on his theories. This characteristic tapestry, from the Alexander series, was dedicated to the king.

Gallery 4 HYACINTHE RIGAUD   *Portrait of Mme de Noailles*
           French, 1659–1743   1692
                                     Oil on canvas
Rigaud, painter to Louis XIV, employed a large workshop, managing to execute about 35 portraits yearly. Insightfully rendered, they also conveyed the opulence of fabrics and trappings.

THAI — *Walking Buddha* — **Gallery 5**
Ayudha Period, 15th c.–18th c. — Bronze
Ayudha Buddhas are copies of images reproduced from legendary likenesses by artists who actually knew the Buddha. They vary little in anatomy, costume and posture. Thai bronzes are fluent and interesting from any angle.

CENTRAL INDIAN — *Vishnu with Attendants* — **Gallery 5**
Benares area — *and Consorts*
12th c.
Sandstone
Benares is a holy city of Hinduism. Over the years princes had temples built of local red sandstone where idols were served by priests and monks. Vishnu is one of the three supreme deities.

JEAN-BAPTISTE CAMILLE COROT — *Dance of the Nymphs* — **Gallery 6**
French, 1796–1875 — Oil on canvas
Corot's romantic landscapes were composed more of tonal variations than of line and color. His most successful paintings were suffused with hazy silvery tones much emulated by later artists.

FRANCIS WHEATLEY — *Crossing the Ford* — **Gallery 8**
British, 1747–1801 — Oil on canvas
Wheatley's graphic genre scenes painted in lucid, delicate color expressed moral attitudes while heeding English sensibilities.

SEVEREIN ROESEN — *A Bountiful Harvest* — **Gallery 9**
Act. U.S., 1848–1871 — Oil on canvas
Roesen painted flowers and sometimes taught. He rendered large pictures of flowers and fruit in detailed style and flamboyant color. Many of his paintings resemble the luscious samples in shop windows.

GEORGIA O'KEEFFE — *Two Jimson Weeds with* — **Gallery 9**
American, b. 1877 — *Green Leaves and Blue Sky*
1938
Oil on canvas
O'Keeffe's close-up views of natural subjects painted in exaggerated, carefully detailed, semiabstract style are sometimes severely cropped, reflecting her earlier association with Stieglitz, the photographer.

MASTER OF THE ALLEGRO — **Gallery 12**
MADONNA — *Madonna and Child with the*
Italian — *Infant Saint John*
Oil on panel
The Master, influenced by Raphael, executed this painting in the High Renaissance style of Florence. At one time it was mistakenly attributed to Piero di Cosimo by Giuseppe Fiocco and Adolfo Ventori. It was attributed to the Master of the Allegro Madonna by Frederico Zeri.

ANDREA VACCARO — *Martha Rebuking Mary Magdalene* — **Gallery 12**
Italian, 1598–1670 — Oil on canvas
Vaccaro was considered the ablest of the Neapolitan School of Painters until Luca Giordano matured. His finest paintings were single figures of saints.

FACILITIES

Gallery Talks, informal introductions to temporary exhibitions and the permanent collection, are offered by the museum staff and guest lecturers.

Changing Exhibitions are regularly featured.

Poetry Readings by prominent contemporary American poets are sponsored during the winter and spring.

Special Performing Events by national and local performers are scheduled during the year.

Films on art are screened each Saturday and Sunday afternoon, 3 P.M.

Metered Parking (2-hour limit) can be found behind the museum.

Hours: Monday–Friday, 10 A.M.–5 P.M.; Saturday–Sunday, 2 P.M.–5 P.M.
Closed: National holidays.

Admission: Free.

SPRINGVILLE

SPRINGVILLE MUSEUM OF ART
126 East 400 South
Springville, UT 84663
Tel: (801)489-9434

The museum was founded in 1903, the present building having been erected in 1935–1937 with WPA money. The Spanish-style two-story structure has exterior walls of troweled stucco masonry and a tile roof. Handmade tile floors and carved oak woodwork enhance the nine exhibition galleries. The collection consists of some 500 works, mostly paintings, some sculpture and other two-dimensional works and includes early 20th-century American art, European works, sculptures by Cyrus Dallin and paintings by Utah artists from the early days to the present.

SAMPLING THE COLLECTION

Upper
Floor

JOSEPH MALLORD WILLIAM
TURNER   *Ship Burning at Sea*
British, 1775–1851   Oil on canvas
Turner's early marine scenes met with great popular acclaim. His later ones were more difficult to accept as they became increasingly abstract dissolving into "tinted steam." He deeply influenced Impressionism.

Upper
Floor

CHILDE HASSAM   *Blue Phantasy*
American, 1859–1935   Oil on canvas
Hassam's impressionistic style was most influenced by Monet. He painted cityscapes and landscapes, attempting to show the effect of sunlight on his subjects.

Exterior view. Courtesy Springville Museum of Art, Springville

WILLIAM SERGEANT KENDALL   *The Artist's Wife and Daughter*   **Upper**
American, 1869–1938   1906   **Floor**
Oil on canvas
Kendall studied painting in the United States and in Paris and became director
of the Yale School of Fine Arts. He is represented in some of the most prestigious
museums in this country.

WILLIAM KEITH   *Landscape*   **Upper**
American, 1839–1911   Oil on canvas   **Floor**
Keith painted mainly California landscapes. His early work consisted of large
panoramic views. Later, influenced by a Swedenborgian minister, he tried to
interpret the inner meaning of nature.

Upper   CYRUS E. DALLIN   *Appeal to the Great Spirit*
Floor   American, 1861–1944   1909
                                                      Bronze

Dallin, a native of Springville, studied in Paris, where he worked with Rosa Bonheur. He is best known for his statues of Indians.

FACILITIES

Concerts are frequently presented.

A small *Library* is available.

The *Sales Shop* carries old pioneer photographs $4–$15; calendars; jewelry from the Metropolitan Museum in New York and from Boston museums, $5–$15, and art books, including one on Cyrus Dallin, $15.

An *Art Rental and Sales Gallery* is sponsored by the museum.

Hours: Tuesday–Saturday, 10 A.M.–5 P.M.; Sunday, 2 P.M.–5 P.M. *Closed:* Mondays.

Admission: Free.

WASHINGTON

BELLINGHAM

WHATCOM MUSEUM OF HISTORY AND ART
121 Prospect St.
Bellingham, WA 98225
Tel: (206)676-6981

The museum was established in 1940 in the former New Whatcom City Hall, which was erected in 1892, some 40 years after the arrival of the first white settlers and 10 years before the town of Bellingham was formed. The red pressed brick and Chuckanut sandstone walls enclose an interior of detailed wood paneling. The building, closed in 1962 to repair the damage from a destructive fire, reopened in 1968 with a restored exterior and an interior remodeled into spacious galleries. The second floor Rotunda Room, once the courtroom, usually features works by regional and nationally known artists. The collection also contains Victorian decorative arts displayed in three turn-of-the-century rooms; American Indian art and artifacts reaching northward from the area to the Aleutians; dioramas, photographs and tools from the logging industry and ornithological examples.

SAMPLING THE COLLECTION

The artworks listed below are rotated for exhibition.

PHILIP MCCRACKEN
American, b. 1928

Heron
1977
Open air bronze sculpture

McCracken's sculptures are often of birds, beasts and totems influenced by his Northwestern surroundings.

MARK TOBEY
American, 1890–1976

Winter Growth
1957
Tempera

Far Eastern religion, American Indian art, Japanese woodcuts and Oriental calligraphy have all influenced Tobey's art. Intricate, delicately patterned "white writings" characterize his paintings of this period.

MORRIS GRAVES
American, b. 1910

Four Fish
1955
Gouache

Graves's gouaches, produced on thin paper, are reminiscent of Oriental scroll-work. He has been influenced by Far Eastern religion and philosophy and also by the "white writings" of Tobey.

GEORGE RICKEY
American, b. 1907

Two Lines Oblique Bellingham
1971
Stainless steel

Rickey's kinetic sculptures are chiefly seen outdoors. His geometric, tapered pieces are finely balanced allowing the least breeze to set them slowly astir, creating a mood of serenity.

Not on   DARIUS KINSEY   *Photographs of Logging*
Permanent   American, 1896–1940
Exhibition Five thousand original negatives and 300 original prints tell the story of the pioneer loggers and the industry that grew out of their efforts. Kinsey took the photographs. His wife, Tabitha, developed them.

FACILITIES

Lectures on art or historical subjects are often presented as are *Concerts* of classical and popular music.

Changing Exhibitions are regularly featured.

Theater Performances include puppet shows and one-act plays.

Dance Programs, Films and *Poetry Readings* are also offered.

Hours: Tuesday–Sunday, 12 P.M.–5 P.M. *Closed:* Mondays, Christmas, New Year's.

Admission: Free.

GOLDENDALE

MARYHILL MUSEUM OF ART
12 miles west of Goldendale
on Highway 14
Goldendale, WA 98620
Tel: (509)773-4792

The museum is located above the Columbia River just a bridge length from the state of Oregon. Conceived by Sam Hill, a wealthy lawyer, and the dancer, Loie Fuller, it was dedicated in 1926 by Queen Marie of Romania who appreciated the aid given to her country by Mr. Hill after World War I. It remained an empty concrete shell until 1940, when it was opened to the public, having been rescued by Alma Spreckels, widow of the sugar tycoon, who gifted it with most of its collection. On view is European and American art, including paintings, sculpture, ceramics and glass; Rodin drawings and sculpture; French manikins; rare and modern chessmen; articles of European royalty and Northwest Indian artifacts.

SAMPLING THE COLLECTION

AUGUSTE RODIN   *Flore*
French, 1840–1917   Painted plaster
Rodin produced this bust in 18th-century style at the outset of his career while also working commercially as a decorative carver.

ALASKAN   *Halibut Hook*
Northwest Coast Indians   Wood
Fishing was an important activity of the Northwest Coast Indians, freeing them
at certain times of the year to indulge in artistic pursuits. Carving was a common
art form.

QUEEN MARIE OF ROMANIA ROOM

This gallery houses the furniture and memorabilia of Queen Marie, a capable
craftswoman, who designed and helped to execute some of the elaborate
pieces.

FACILITIES

Lectures and *Concerts* are presented. Write for program information to Star
Route 677, Goldendale, WA 98620.

The *Gift Shop* sells mostly souvenir booklets, postcards, and petroglyphs, ceramics, icons, baskets and gifts related to the Maryhill collections.

Hours: Daily, March 15–November 15, 9 A.M.–5 P.M.

Admission: Adults, $1.50; senior adults, $1; students, 50¢; children under 6,
             free.

SEATTLE

CHARLES AND EMMA FRYE ART MUSEUM
Terry and Cherry
Seattle, WA 98114
Tel: (206)622-9250

The museum was opened in 1952, a gift from the Fryes to the city of Seattle.
Three galleries display the permanent collection, representing primarily paintings from the Munich School covering the period 1850–1925.

SAMPLING THE COLLECTION

FRANZ VON LENBACH   *Count Von Moltke*   **Gallery A-10**
German, 1836–1904   Oil on canvas
Von Moltke was a hero of the 1870 war. Lenbach, the outstanding portraitist
of his time, stressed the head. The 15 Lenbachs in the museum make this the
largest collection of Lenbachs in America.

ALEXANDER MAX KOESTER   *Enten (Ducks)*   **Gallery A-12**
German, 1864–1932   Oil on canvas
Koester was a painter of mood landscapes. He often painted ducks and was
skillful in capturing the effects of light and shadow on the feathers.

MAX LIEBERMANN   *Dutch Courtyard*   **Gallery B-17**
German, 1847–1935   Oil on canvas
Liebermann spent a good deal of time in Holland. It was there that he painted
his first plein air canvases and, subsequently, became one of the leaders of
German Impressionism.

Eugène Louis Boudin, View of Harbor, Havre. *Courtesy Charles and Emma Frye Art Museum, Seattle*

Gallery B-28   JOHAN JONGKIND   *Moonlight Scene*
Dutch, 1819–1891   Oil on canvas
Jongkind's landscapes and marine paintings profoundly influenced the early Impressionists. This painting catches the feeling of the texture and movement of sky and clouds. He was a lonely man unappreciated in his time.

Gallery B-34   EUGENE LOUIS BOUDIN   *View of Harbor, Havre*
French, 1824–1898   Oil on canvas
Boudin knew the coastline from the northern tip of France to the end of the Norman peninsula intimately. He caught the subdued colors, the haze, the shadings of blue, blue-gray and green.

Gallery C-28   FRANZ VON STUCK   *Sin*
German, 1863–1928   Oil on canvas
Sin created a great stir in Berlin. Stuck thought he had found the simplest expression of sin with this nude woman contrasted against a dark background, with the serpent, the symbol of sin, wound about the body.

FACILITIES

Changing Exhibitions are regularly featured.

A *Gallery Guidebook* is available at 15¢. It is detailed and helpful.

A *Sales Desk* offers color postcards of museum paintings, 10¢ each, and a museum catalog, $1.

Hours: Monday–Saturday, 10 A.M.–5 P.M.; Sundays, holidays, 12 P.M.–6 P.M.
         Closed: Thanksgiving, Christmas.
Admission: Free.

HENRY ART GALLERY, UNIVERSITY OF WASHINGTON
15th Ave. N.E. at Northeast 41st St.
Seattle, WA 98195
Tel: (206)543-2280

The university's gallery, opened on the campus in 1927, was a gift from Seattle railroad magnate, Horace C. Henry. Built in a modified Tudor Gothic design, the varied patterns of its brick exterior are divided by stone, ornamented in low relief. Seven galleries house the collection of works by Pacific Northwest artists, including 91 drawings and paintings by Morris Graves and 35 by Mark Tobey; 19th-and 20th-century American and European paintings; contemporary American ceramics and African art. The greatest areas of strength lie in the collection's American and European drawings and prints and in its contemporary Japanese folk art.

SAMPLING THE COLLECTION

WILLIAM HOGARTH   *Gin Lane*
British, 1697–1764   1751
                            Engraving
Hogarth's satirical engravings are moral commentaries on 18th-century English life. Handling his subjects as a playwright might, he hoped they would be judged by the same criteria.

GIOVANNI BATTISTA PIRANESI *Hadrian's Villa: The*
Italian, 1720–1778   *Canopus Interior*
                            1776
                            Etching
Piranesi's romantic architectural etchings of ancient and modern Rome were executed with outstanding draftsmanship and dramatic contrasts in shading. For many they provided the definitive image of that city.

GEORGES ROUAULT   *Miserere*
French, 1871–1958   Heliogravure with etching and
                            engraving
Rouault's pictures were inspired by Catholicism and a deep sensitivity to man's suffering. Broad black outlines and heavy forms are evidence of his early training as a stained glass apprentice.

WINSLOW HOMER   *An Adirondack Lake*
American, 1836–1910   1870
                            Oil on canvas
This is the second version Homer rendered of *An Adirondack Lake.* It is larger, more formally composed, showing smoother brushwork. Nature is the predominating theme in much of Homer's work.

MARK TOBEY   *Untitled*
American, 1890–1976   1964
                                    Monoprint, tempera on paper
Tobey, devoted to the Bahai faith, sought to blend Oriental techniques with
Western ones. His calligraphic pictures of overall design presaged the drip
paintings of Jackson Pollock although both had individual origins.

MORRIS GRAVES   *Chalice with Moon*
American, b. 1910   Tempera on paper
Graves has been influenced by Eastern religion and philosophy, by Northwest
Indian mythology and by Mark Tobey. His methods are akin to Oriental scroll
painting while his "white writing" reflects Tobey's work.

SHOJI HAMADA   *Large Bowl*
Japanese, b. 1894   ca. 1950
                                    Stoneware
Hamada is the leading mingo (folk art) potter in Japan. He produces heavy,
rather coarse-looking ware in somber colors that are typically Japanese, using
abstract decorative designs.

FACILITIES

Lectures on art and related subjects are presented.

Symposia on art featuring noted authorities are arranged from time to time.

Temporary Exhibitions culled from the art gallery's collection or *Loan Exhibitions* from other institutions are regular features of the museum's program.

Hours: Monday–Friday, 10 A.M.–5 P.M.; Thursday, 7 P.M.–9 P.M.; Saturday–
         Sunday, 1 P.M.–5 P.M.. *Closed:* University holidays.

Admission: Free.

SEATTLE ART MUSEUM
Volunteer Park
Seattle, WA 98112

MODERN ART PAVILION
Seattle Center
2nd and Thomas
Seattle, WA 98112
Tel: (206)447-4710

The museum was constructed in Volunteer Park in 1933. It is a fine example
of *art moderne* style of the 1930s. The building today is regarded as a distinctive example of Art Deco. From the museum Puget Sound can be seen with
snow-covered mountains behind it. The collection includes Egyptian, Greek,
Roman, Gothic, Renaissance and Baroque painting and sculpture; pre-Columbian and African art; painting and sculpture of the American Northwest; decorative arts; textiles; and graphics, and is especially strong in Oriental art. In
addition to the Volunteer Park facility, the Modern Art Pavilion is located on

Tawaraya Sōtatsu, Deer and Poems. *From the collection of the Seattle Art Museum, Seattle*

the Seattle site of the 1962 "Century 21" World's Fair. It was formerly the United Kingdom and Republic of China Pavilions. The contemporary collection is displayed here.

SAMPLING THE COLLECTION

JAPANESE Momoyama Period, 1568–1615	*Ewer* early 17th c. Mino ware, Oribe-type stoneware with copper green and transparent glazes over painted iron brown decoration	**Gallery N1**

The tea master, Furuta Oribe, originated a daring design in tea ceremony ceramics. Possibly his samurai past influenced the boldness and drama of his work.

UNKOKU TOGAN Japanese, 1547–1617	*Eight Views of Hsiao-Hsiang* (Shōshō Hakkei) Part of sixfold screens in ink on paper	**Gallery N1**

This popular theme, called Shōshō Hakkei, where the Hsiao and Hsiang rivers converge, depicts the rivers' varied moods. Four of eight views are shown on this pair of screens from the late Muromachi to early Momoyama periods.

TAWARAYA SOTATSU, PAINTER Japanese, 1576–1643	*Deer and Poems* (detail) early 17th c.	**Gallery N1,** **Displayed** **Annually in** **June or July**
HONAMI KOETSU, POET Japanese, 1558–1637	Hand scroll in ink, gold and silver on paper	

This joint effort, created in the Edo period, is based on a practice from the Heian period, an earlier time, when poetry and painting were combined to express a totally Japanese form of art.

JAPANESE Late Kofun Period, 6th c.	*Haniwa Warrior* Reddish pottery with traces of polychrome decoration	**Gallery N3**

This cylindrical grave figure was one of many that surmounted the cylindrical tiles (Haniwa) marking the gravesites of dead overlords. They are undoubtedly the most important work of prehistoric Japan.

Gallery N4   CHINESE   *Armenoid Merchant Holding*
             T'ang Dynasty, A.D. 618–906   *Wine Skin*
                                                      8th c.
                                                      Pottery with san ts'ai (three color)
                                                      glaze
This foreign merchant, among the many strangers in China during an active
trading period, has a belly virtually indistinguishable from his wine sack, indicat-
ing the levity with which the Chinese viewed these outsiders.

Gallery N4   HSUEH CH'UANG   *Orchids in First Bloom*
             Chinese, 1260–1368,   1345
             act. mid-14th c.   Hanging scroll in ink on silk
The painter was a Ch'an monk. Floral themes were used in Ch'an Buddhism for
the contemplation and understanding of nature. The Ch'an stressed individual-
ism, therefore each brush stroke was controlled and significant.

Gallery N4   CHINESE   *Buddhist Monk*
             Yüan Dynasty, 1260–1368   Wood with polychrome decoration
The Lin-chi sect of Ch'an religion stressed the individual's ultimate abrupt
enlightenment. One can feel the anguish and conflict thought to be experienced
when the spirit triumphs over man's ignorance.

Jade Room   KOREAN   *Vase (mae byŏng)*
             Kŏryŏ Period, 918–1392   late 12th–early 13th c.
                                                      Porcelaneous ware with incised
                                                      decoration and transparent, grayish
                                                      green celadon glaze
The shape of this vase is well suited to hold a single spray of prunus blossom,
which lends its name (mae byŏng) to the vase.

Jade Room   CHINESE   *Disc (pi)*
             Chou Dynasty, ca. 1027–256 B.C.   Jade
The *pi*, a disk with a center hole, is the symbol of heaven. This *pi* is of jade,
a gemstone believed to prolong life.

Garden   INDIAN   *Devī*
Court   Deogarh Style   late 6th c.
                                                      Sandstone
Devī was the ideal mother and consort. The striations on this sculpture are
distinguishing marks of the Deogarh style.

Garden   THAI   *Buddha*
Court   Dvāravatī Style,   7th–8th c.
             Mon-Gupta Type   Grayish blue limestone
Religious sculpture in Thailand was dominated by Buddha. The Dvāravatī style
was a simplified version of the Gupta in which the sculptor smoothed the body
connections.

Garden   SOUTH INDIAN   *Shiva as Teacher of Music*
Court   Chola Period, mid-9th c.–ca. 1310   (Vinadharadaksina-murti)
                                                      10th c.
                                                      Bronze
Shiva, an important Hindu deity whose cosmic dance of creation and destruc-
tion were often created in sculpture, was also a music teacher. Typical of Chola
sculpture are the large head and generous features.

JACKSON POLLOCK American, 1912–1956	*Sea Change* 1947 Collage of oil and small pebbles on canvas	**Modern Art Pavilion**

Pollock is most famous for his drip paintings. Paint was dripped or poured in a seemingly haphazard manner extending to the ends of enormous canvases enveloping the viewer.

ARSHILE GORKY Armenian/American, 1904–1948	*How My Mother's Embroidered* *Apron Unfolds in My Life* 1944 Oil on canvas	**Modern Art Pavilion**

Gorky's work was influenced by Picasso, grounded in European Surrealism and evolved into Abstract Expressionism. His later paintings marked by light colors and black brush strokes had a visceral quality.

MARK TOBEY American, 1890–1976	*Parnassus* 1963 Oil on canvas	**Modern Art Pavilion**

Tobey was influenced by Oriental religion and calligraphy. His "white writings" are overall calligraphic and labyrinthine works reminiscent of Pollock's drip paintings. However, both artists were differently motivated.

GUY ANDERSON American, b. 1906	*Spring (Stop the Bomb)* 1967 Newspaper collage and oil on paper on wood	**Modern Art Pavilion**

Anderson is a significant Northwestern artist whose early paintings, mainly landscapes with figures, displayed an interest in Cubism. In his later work, this is integrated with Northwest Indian elements.

FACILITIES

Tours conducted by trained guides are offered at the Volunteer Park Museum daily at 2 P.M. and at the Modern Art Pavilion on Thursdays, Saturdays, and Sundays at 2 P.M.

Group Tours may be arranged by calling the tour desk (206)447-4708.

Lectures on art or related subjects are frequently held.

Temporary Exhibitions culled from the museum's collection or *Loan Exhibitions* from other institutions are regular features of the museum's program.

Special Events for senior citizens are offered free of charge on the first Friday of each month.   **Volunteer Park**

Films on a variety of subjects in the art field are featured.

The *Art Reference Library* is open Tuesday–Friday, 10 A.M.–12 P.M., 1:30 P.M.– 5 P.M.   **Volunteer Park**

The *Slide Library* is open Monday–Friday, 9 A.M.–12 P.M., 1 P.M.–5 P.M.

The *Sales Shop's* most popular items are the art catalogs of exhibitions and of the museum's permanent collection.   **Volunteer Park**

Modern Art   *Rentaloft* sells or rents artworks featuring the work of Northwestern artists.
Pavilion
Hours: *Volunteer Park:* Tuesday–Saturday, 10 A.M.–5 P.M.; Sundays, holidays,
12 P.M.–5 P.M.; Thursday evenings, 8 P.M.–10 P.M. *Closed:* Mondays.
Modern Art Pavilion: Tuesday–Sunday, 11 A.M.–6 P.M.; Thursday eve-
nings, 6 P.M.–8 P.M.; *Closed:* Mondays.

Admission: Adults, $1; students and senior citizens, 50¢; children under 12
free when accompanied by an adult. Thursdays are free.

TACOMA

TACOMA ART MUSEUM
12th and Pacific Ave.
Tacoma, WA 98402
Tel: (206)272-4258

The Neoclassic-style museum was founded in 1890 and is located in the heart
of downtown Tacoma. The collection concentrates on American 20th-century
art and is strongest in its examples of paintings from the American "Eight."

SAMPLING THE COLLECTION

MAURICE PRENDERGAST   *Coast Scene at Newport,*
American, 1859–1924   *Rhode Island*
1905
Watercolor

Although Prendergast, one of "The Eight," worked in other mediums, he is best
known for his watercolors. His simple strong compositions are rendered in
flecked color, influenced by French Neo-Impressionism.

WILLIAM GLACKENS   *Natalie in a Blue Skirt*
American, 1870–1938   1914
Oil

Glackens executed still lifes and genre scenes in the manner of "The Eight."
From 1914 on he turned to nudes and portraits, using a rosy palette influenced
by Renoir.

EVERETT SHINN   *Ballet in the Park*
American, 1876–1953   Oil

Shinn, who briefly joined "The Eight," was originally an illustrator. He later
became a theatrical decorator and portraitist. Ballet dancers were a favored
subject.

JEAN DUBUFFET   *Palmiers aux Oiseaux*
French, b. 1901   1948
Gouache

Dubuffet's simple subjects are influenced by the art of children and psychotics
in which he finds true artistic expression.

ANDREW WYETH
American, b. 1917

Braddock's Coat
1969
Mixed media

Wyeth confines his subject matter to depictions of the people and locales in and around his rural Northeastern homes. A feeling of isolation and sadness pervades his meticulously rendered work.

FACILITIES

Temporary Exhibitions culled from the museum's collection or *Loan Exhibitions* from other institutions are regular features of the museum's program.

The *Children's Gallery* contains a special exhibition that instructs by means of a puppet show, a narrative guided tour and a slide presentation of historical information.

The *Bookshop* sells art-related books and gifts.

The *Art Rental Gallery* is open Mondays and Wednesdays, 10 A.M.–4 P.M. or by appointment.

The *Early American Room* re-creates an 18th-century American living room **3rd Floor** with original furniture and decorative arts of the period. Open Monday–Friday, 10 A.M.–4 P.M..

The *Sara Little Center for Design Research* features old and new functional and **3rd Floor** historic design items from around the world. Open Monday, Friday, Sunday, 10 A.M.–4 P.M..

Hours: Monday–Saturday, 10 A.M.–4 P.M.; Sunday, 12 P.M.–5 P.M. *Closed·* Major holidays.

Admission: Free.

BIG HORN

BRADFORD BRINTON MEMORIAL MUSEUM
Big Horn, WY 82833
Tel: (307)672-3173

The museum, a National Historic Site, was opened in 1961 on the grounds of the Quarter Circle A Ranch. It is typical of the prosperous ranches of the area settled in the 1870s and 1880s. Built in 1892 as a home, its second owner, Bradford Brinton, filled it with fine furniture, Western art, Indian handcrafts, old and rare books and historic documents. The Reception Gallery, the only non-ranch building, serves as an exhibit area in which the material is changed yearly. Other outbuildings include saddle and carriage barns and the Little Goose Lodge, a log cabin.

Main Ranch House. *Courtesy Bradford Brinton Memorial Museum, Big Horn*

SAMPLING THE COLLECTION

CHARLES MARION RUSSELL   *When Ropes Go Wrong*
American, 1864–1926   1925
                                Watercolor

Russell, the "Cowboy Artist," spent his early years as a cowhand in Montana and became one of the better-known artists of the Western cowboy.

FREDERIC REMINGTON   *Flight on the Little Big Horn*   **Main House,**
American, 1861–1909   ca. 1890s   **Living Room**
                            Oil

                            Indian Encampment   **Living Room**
                            ca. 1891
                            Oil

                            Going to Pierre Hole Fight   **Music Room**
                            ca. 1890s
                            Oil

Remington's paintings, sculptures and illustrations depicted the Old West with accurate detail. The above were accomplished in his mature years, in black and white, probably as illustrations for magazine articles.

FACILITIES

Tours are offered daily until 4:15 P.M.   **Reception**

Lectures and *Demonstrations* are held from time to time.   **Gallery**

A *Gift Shop* features reproductions of Western artists, original art, books, and other reproductions from national sources.

Hours: *Daily, May 15 to Labor Day:* 9 A.M.–5 P.M. *By written appointment during the rest of the year.*

Admission: Free.

CODY

BUFFALO BILL HISTORICAL CENTER
8th and Sheridan Ave.
Cody, WY 82414
Tel: (307)587-4771

PLAINS INDIAN MUSEUM

The center opened in 1927 in an ordinary log cabin. Today, in low-lying stone buildings set against a mountain landscape not far from the Eastern Entrance of

Exterior view. Buffalo Bill Historical Center, Cody

Yellowstone National Park, it encompasses four museums providing a comprehensive view of our nation's Western history. In addition to the Plains Indian Museum and Whitney Gallery, the Buffalo Bill Museum tells William F. Cody's exhilarating life story, while the Winchester Museum, located for over a century in New Haven, Connecticut, exhibits an extensive collection of arms from the earliest times onward.

WHITNEY GALLERY OF WESTERN ART

Established in 1958 with one of this country's most inclusive collections of paintings and sculpture, the gallery traces Western life from the earliest recordings of George Catlin and Karl Bodmer to the later work of Frederic Remington, Charles Russell and their contemporaries to today's artists of the Western school.

SAMPLING THE COLLECTION

BUFFALO BILL HISTORICAL CENTER

FREDERIC REMINGTON   *The Night Herder*
American, 1861–1909   Oil on canvas
Remington, a cowboy and rancher, later produced writings, illustrations, paintings, and sculptures of cowboys and Indians. Although he died at forty-eight, he completed over 3,000 works on the West.

PLAINS INDIAN MUSEUM

By exhibiting the art and utilitarian objects of the Plains Indians, the museum preserves the culture and traditions of these Native Americans.

CROW   *Horse's Neck Decoration*
                              ca. 1860–1870
                              Skunkhide
Designs on horse trappings as well as those on robes, shirts and moccasins endowed their owners with prestige.

CHEYENNE   *Moccasins*
                              ca. 1880–1890
                              Beaded soles
Geometric decorative designs were always introduced by the women, the men were solely responsible for naturalistic ornamentation.

WHITNEY GALLERY OF WESTERN ART

ALBERT BIERSTADT   *Yellowstone Falls*
American, 1830–1902   after 1859
                              Oil on canvas
Bierstadt's romantically exaggerated and theatrically lit canvases of Western landscapes had immense appeal for many who eagerly accepted his grandiose renditions. He enjoyed great popularity.

CHARLES MARION RUSSELL   *Attack on the Wagon Train*
American, 1864–1926   Oil on canvas
Before Russell became a painter he worked as a cowhand, gaining firsthand knowledge of the cowboys whose lives he later depicted in romantic renditions.

FACILITIES

The *Library's* shelves reflect the major themes of the museum—Western art, history, Indians and firearms.

The *Museum Shop* sells books, slides, cookbooks, postcards, posters and catalogs relating to the collection.

Hours: *May and September:* Daily, 8 A.M.–5 P.M. *June–August:* Daily, 7 A.M.–
         10 P.M.

Admission: Adults, $2.50; ages 6–15, $1.

LARAMIE

UNIVERSITY OF WYOMING ART MUSEUM
19th and Willet
Fine Arts Center
Laramie, WY 82070
Tel: (307)766-2374

This university museum shares its quarters with the music and theater departments. The museum consists of two galleries. The larger one overlooks the central court of the complex complete with sculpture, plantings and a fountain. The collection is composed of paintings, graphics and sculpture, its greatest strength lying in 19th- and 20th-century American art.

SAMPLING THE COLLECTION

The collection is exhibited on a rotating basis so that these works may not always be on view.

FREDERICK MACMONNIES   *Bacchante with Infant Faun*
American, 1863–1937   1894
                              Bronze
MacMonnies was a pupil of Saint-Gaudens. His skillfully executed, occasionally superficial, public monuments are his best work.

JOHN GEORGE BROWN   *The Conspirators*
British/American, 1831–1913   1904
                              Oil on canvas
Brown portrayed incidents of daily life simply and realistically. Because of his concern for the effects of light on a composition, he often placed his figures in sunny landscape settings.

THOMAS MORAN   *Grand Canal, Venice*
American, 1837–1926   Oil
Moran, a member of the later Hudson River School, was a successful painter of large landscapes.

THEODOR ROMBOUTS   *The Concert*
Flemish, 1597–1637   Oil
Rombouts was influenced by Caravaggio on a visit to Italy but later abandoned this style to adopt one closer to Rubens. He, himself, had many students.

ALFRED STEVENS   *Femme aux Fleurs*
Belgian, 1828–1906   Oil on canvas
Stevens frequented the court of Empress Eugenie and painted in the Realist style popular under the French Second Empire.

FACILITIES

Lectures and *Films* on art-related subjects are frequently offered.

Changing Exhibitions are regularly featured.

The *Reception Desk* sells postcards and catalogs.

Hours: Sunday–Friday, 1:30 P.M.–5 P.M. *Closed:* Saturdays.

Admission: Free.

ROCK SPRINGS

SWEETWATER COMMUNITY FINE ARTS CENTER
40 C St.
Rock Springs, WY 82901
Tel: (307)382-4599

The center, opened in 1966, displays over 200 works of art owned by the Rock Springs High School. They were donated by a former instructor.

SAMPLING THE COLLECTION

NORMAN ROCKWELL
American, 1894–1973

New Year's Eve
ca. 1943
Oil

Rockwell, a successful magazine illustrator at age nineteen, continued to record American life in the 20th century. Among his most popular themes have been growing up, young love and patriotism.

GRANDMA MOSES
(ANNA MARY ROBERTSON MOSES)
American, 1860–1961

Staunton, Virginia
1946
Oil

Grandma Moses began painting at age seventy-six. Her lively, naïve depictions of 19th-century small-town and farm life were immediately successful.

RAPHAEL SOYER
Russian/American, 1899–1974

Girl in Brown Jacket
ca. 1941
Oil

Soyer painted realistic interpretations of city life. In the following decades he brightened his palette but continued to ignore the new directions of modern art movements.

FACILITIES

Lectures, Demonstrations, Musical and *Dramatic* performances are all offered from time to time.

Hours: *Winter:* Wednesday–Friday, 1 P.M.–5 P.M.; 6:30 P.M.–8:30 P.M.; Saturdays, 2 P.M.–5 P.M. *Summer:* Wednesday–Friday, 10 A.M.–12 P.M., 2 P.M.–5 P.M., 6:30 P.M.–8:30 P.M. *Closed:* Sundays.

Admission: Free.

GLOSSARY

ABSTRACT EXPRESSIONISM was a name given to the post-World War II art movement that was nonrepresentational and feeling and in which the subconscious was given free reign. It comprised two methods: Action Painting and Abstract-Image Painting. See **COLOR FIELD PAINTING**.

ABSTRACT-IMAGE PAINTING. See **COLOR FIELD PAINTING**.

ACTION PAINTING. A term describing a brand of Abstract Expressionism practiced by Jackson Pollock, Willem de Kooning, etc. Paint is dripped and splashed on the canvas in an unrestrained manner, the accidental being used to advantage.

ANALYTICAL CUBISM was the first phase of Cubism. It was explored by Picasso and Braque from 1907 to 1912 and based on Cézanne's handling of nature "in terms of the cylinder, the sphere and the cone." They sought to convey subjects in the round as a totality without diminishing the value of the picture's flat surface.

ART DECO is a design and decorative arts style associated with the 1920s and 1930s. Exotic decorations and streamlined geometric designs, influenced by Cubism, permeated architecture, interior and industrial design, graphics and crafts.

ART NOUVEAU was an international style popular in the 1890s in architecture, the applied arts and interior design. Highly stylized, it emphasized intricate organic themes.

ASHCAN SCHOOL. See **THE EIGHT**.

BARBIZON SCHOOL was composed of a group of French landscapists who settled at the edge of the forest of Fontainebleau in the village of Barbizon and fostered landscape painting as an expression of art important in its own right.

BAROQUE ART, originating in Italy, especially Rome, was dominant in Western Europe, ca. 1580–ca. 1720. It is marked by dynamic, intensely emotional expression, dramatic lighting, asymmetry and compositions that seemingly extend into space. Individual effects are dominated by the whole.

CHAMPAGNE SCHOOL appeared in Champagne, France, toward the close of the 15th century and the opening of the 16th century. It favored the simple, serious Gothic style of earlier times and was especially popular among the rich middle class.

CHIPPENDALE is a furniture style of the mid-18th century that mirrors the French Rococo. Mahogany chairs with pierced complex splats typify these designs as does ornately carved furniture of Chinese and Gothic influence, some of which are carved, japanned or gilded. Commencing in the 1760s luxuriously carved pieces became classical in design.

CLASSICISM in art implies reason, order, restraint and harmony based on models and principles descended from ancient Greece and Rome.

CLOISSONNISME. See **SYNTHETISM**.

COLOR FIELD PAINTING evolved in the 1950s and is known interchangeably as Post-Painterly Abstraction, Cool Art and Abstract-Image Painting. Rejecting drawing, optical illusion, motion, light and figuration these artists were concerned with simple, flat, brilliantly colored areas and general form concentrating on the act of painting itself.

CONSTRUCTIVISM, essentially a nonobjective, three-dimensional art most commonly seen in sculpture, also appears in paintings and graphics. Originating in Russia in the 1920s, its proponents employed modern technological materials such as plastic, iron and wire.

CUBISM, begun by Picasso and Braque about 1907, became the watershed from which many abstract styles developed. It was derived from Cézanne's later work in which he attempted to control space and light in geometric forms and from African sculpture with its faceted surfaces, stylization and simple forms. Cubism consists of two phases—**ANALYTICAL CUBISM** and **SYNTHETIC CUBISM.**

DADAISM was a precursor of **SURREALISM,** an international movement popular from about 1916 to 1923. Its center was in Zurich but it was also developed in New York and Paris. Disillusioned by World War I, these artists attacked tradition in all forms, expressing themselves with irreverence and absurdity.

THE EIGHT were artists Arthur Davies, William Glackens, Ernest Lawson, George Luks, Maurice Prendergast, Everett Shinn, John Sloan, led by Robert Henri. In 1907, they defected from the National Academy of Design to exhibit together. Most of them painted realistic pictures of the sordid life of the city, although some conveyed its pleasant aspects. Even though their styles were individual, they used predominantly dark colors and unidealized subjects, hence they were referred to in the 1930s as the **ASHCAN SCHOOL.**

EMPIRE STYLE in furniture and decoration was created in France in the early 19th century. It combines Neoclassicism with archeological details made popular after Napoleon's Egyptian campaign.

EXPRESSIONISM is an art form characterized by distortion and exaggeration because the artist concerned themselves with emotional expressions stemming from their inner feelings, rather than depictions of nature or rational subject matter. Greatly influenced by van Gogh, it began in France about 1905 but appeared in other European countries at about the same time. It reached its climax in movements that flourished in Germany.

LES FAUVES, meaning "the wild beasts," was a sobriquet bestowed on a group of artists whose work was shown in 1905 at the Salon d'Automne. Their paintings were distorted, executed in vivid color and composed of bold brush strokes.

FRENCH RESTORATION refers to the restoration of the Bourbons to the French throne in 1815 after the downfall of Napoleon. Neoclassicism yielded to Romanticism. In painting, dramatic lighting, color and contemporary subject matter were featured as exemplified by work of Baron Antoine Jean Gros.

FUTURISM, an early 20th-century movement in literature and art, flourished mainly in Italy commencing in 1910. The painters, in revolt against the past, tried to convey the excitement and motion of the scientific present. Their subjects were things of motion—wheels, legs, fast-moving vehicles. They painted multiple images and used color to achieve a feeling of motion.

GENRE refers to paintings whose subject matter is everyday life. It was a particularly popular mode of expression with 17th-century Dutch painters.

GEORGIAN STYLE applies to architecture, furniture and decorative work produced in England from 1714 to 1820. Organic, unified forms were employed on a small scale. About 1750 the French influenced the simpler English designs introducing Rococo decorations.

GOTHIC predominated in art and architecture in Northern Europe from about 1140 until the 16th century. In Italy it was replaced by the **RENAISSANCE** in the 14th century. Some of its main architectural features are the pointed arch, vaulting buttresses and flying buttresses, stained glass and slender vertical piers, the combination resulting in a soaring skyward monumentality. Humanism and spatial effects appeared in painting.

GOTHIC INTERNATIONAL STYLE was a phase of Gothic art, and appeared in the late 14th and early 15th centuries. It emphasized naturalism, often in secular subjects, refined color and graceful lines.

HUDSON RIVER SCHOOL of painters were 19th-century landscapists who painted romantic interpretations of American scenery concentrating mostly on the Catskill Mountains fringing the Hudson River. They varied in their outlooks from intimate poetic expressions to lofty imaginative ones.

IMPRESSIONISM orginated in the 1870s in France in opposition to academicism. Middle-class subjects were portrayed in broken brush strokes of pure color. The Impressionists sought to capture the evanescence of light and atmosphere on canvas while projecting the greatest naturalism.

INTIMISM is a type of painting practiced in the late 19th century concerned with mainly intimate interior scenes and objects providing a feeling of warmth and security.

MANNERISM, a painting style prominent from about 1520 to 1600, revolted against the classicism of High Renaissance art. Its emotional expression appears in often violent color, elongated figures and distorted exaggerations.

MINIMALISM is an impersonal, precise and restrained art style relying on color and form for its expression.

MUNICH SCHOOL was founded in the second half of the 19th century under the patronage of King Ludwig I of Bavaria. In an effort to enhance the prestige of German art, the school imitated the monumental mural painting of the Italian Renaissance.

NEOCLASSICISM is an artistic and architectural style that predominated ca. 1770–ca. 1830. With the unearthing of Pompeii and Herculaneum and the ensuing interest in antiquity, a reaction against Baroque and Rococo styles occurred. This ordered and restrained style paid attention to accurate detail gleaned from material yielded by the excavations.

NEW YORK SCHOOL. See ABSTRACT EXPRESSIONISM.

OP (OPTICAL ART), a movement of the 1960s, uses graphic devices and the placement of line, pattern and color to create visual distortions that result in illusions to the eye.

POINTILLISM was invented by Seurat in the 1880s. It is a scientifically based method of painting in which small dabs of pure complementary color are placed next to each other and fuse in the eye of the beholder.

POP ART, a movement of the 1960s, originated in England somewhat earlier than the more dynamic American version. It deals with popular and commercial subjects, isolating them in a way that demands that the observer reinspect his surroundings.

POST-IMPRESSIONISM is a loose term generally used to describe the art of Cézanne, Gauguin, van Gogh and others whose varied styles succeeded French Impressionist painting.

PRECISIONISM employs a realistic, often photographic style with flat areas of color and smooth finishes. It evolved in the 1920s, influenced by the geometry and frugal detail of Cubism.

PRE-RAPHAELITE BROTHERHOOD was a group who aimed to study nature and portray events in all honesty regardless of how undecorative the results. They tried to recapture the purity of art before the Renaissance and Raphael who was, they considered, too scientific in his approach.

QUEEN ANNE is a furniture and architectural style that was popular in the first half of the 18th century and originated in England. Marked by Oriental and Classical influences, it is simply carved in mahogany or walnut. Its curved legs end in ornamental feet.

REGIONALISM refers to the work of American painters of the 1930s who depicted life in particular geographical sections. A large number of these artists were from the Midwest and produced pictures of small rural communities there.

RENAISSANCE art began in 14th-century Italy and was adopted throughout Europe yielding, in the early 16th century, to the beginning of modernism. The Early Renaissance, prior to about 1500, was distinguished by humanism and an interest in realism. The climax of the High Renaissance, ca. 1495–ca. 1520, added to these the Classical ideals of harmony and balance.

REPRESENTATIONAL ART, unlike Abstract and Nonobjective art, seeks to duplicate an object or figure fairly closely.

ROCOCO art and decoration originated in 18th-century France and was disseminated throughout Europe. Marked by elegance, gaiety, animation and high color, it is also distinguished by curves, scrollwork and asymmetry.

ROMANESQUE STYLE appeared about the middle of the 11th century and began to decline at the end of the 12th century. It was an eclectic style that drew from Byzantine, Roman, Carolingian and barbarian sources. The details of its architecture are best observed in its massive monasteries that were simple and ordered. The sculpture was linear and angular, often distorted to allow the architecture to accommodate it. Paintings of the period were mostly murals that reflected the same influences as the sculpture and architecture.

ROMANTICISM first emerged in the late 18th century and attained its greatest popularity in the first third of the 19th century. Appearing in art and literature it was fed by the imagination and emotions. It could be subjective and rebellious or manifested in a love of nature and primitive or common man. It often showed an interest in the exotic.

SCHOOL OF FONTAINEBLEAU. The more illustrious First School of Fontainebleau, ca. 1530–ca. 1560, refers to the Mannerist paintings and decorations executed by Italian artists who worked in France for Francis I on the Palace of Fontainebleau. The Second School, during the second half of the century, saw an effort by mainly French artists to continue this work.

SCHOOL OF PARIS refers to the international artists who worked in Paris from about 1900 on. Attracted by the freedom offered by the city for discussion and exhibition, in comparison to other European cities, their art was avantgarde and generally abstract.

SPONTANEOUS STYLE. A popular style of painting at the close of the Sung Dynasty (1127–1279) which combined the shorthand techniques of earlier scholar painters and calligraphers with the older Lyric Style. It added a feeling for nature and man derived from Taoism and Ch'an Buddhism.

SURREALISM emerged ca. 1922 and owes its origins partly to Dadaism and Cubism. It attempts to fuse the dream world with the real one demanding that the artist free himself from his usual means of expression and devote himself to his subconscious and the irrational.

SYNCHROMISM was developed in 1913 in Paris by the Americans Stanton MacDonald-Wright and Morgan Russell. It depended on planes of color and their relationships.

SYNTHETIC CUBISM, the second phase of Cubism, incorporated printed and other collage material on its plane surfaces reintroducing color and subject.

SYNTHETISM, or Cloisonnisme, is a painting method that expresses the emotions rather than duplicating the observable. Its artificial appearance helps to convey the intangible. Flattened, two-dimensional areas are encompassed by broad curved outlines of high color resembling stained glass painting or cloisonné enamel.

THE TEN were a group of American, mostly Impressionist painters, who exhibited together from 1895 on.

VICTORIAN art and architecture were so named for the style popular during the reign of England's Queen Victoria (1837–1901). Rococo and Renaissance styles were adapted to mass production manifested in showy, ornamented pieces.

WASHINGTON COLOR PAINTERS were a group who exhibited in the Washington, D.C. Gallery of Modern Art in 1965. Interested in the optical effects of color that could be achieved through geometric, largely hard-edged repeated designs, they usually painted in series to stress the changeability and property of the colors.

WILLIAM AND MARY period of furniture design, popular ca. 1690–ca. 1730, echoed the Baroque style of the earlier 1600s. Contrasting wood grains were used and columnar supports became more delicate.

INDEX OF ARTISTS